D0228764

A BOOK OF ENGLISH IDIOMS

Mr. Collins, renowned champion of the English language against misuse, presents a collection of idioms employed most frequently today. The success of the first edition, the author states, has given him gratifying opportunity, much sooner than he had dared to hope, of seeing incorporated in a second and a third edition a number of corrections and revisions. It has also encouraged him to compile a sequel entitled *A Second Book of English Idioms*.

The book will be of great value to all who wish to use contemporary English expertly and intelligently, whether in speech or writing. A majority of the corrections and revisions have been made as a direct result of the many criticisms offered not only by Mr. Collins's friends but by strangers who have written to him.

Mr. Collins's other books, *The Choice of Words*, *One Word and Another*, and *Right Word, Wrong Word*, have been highly praised by many contemporary critics of the spoken and written word, and he worthily maintains in this new edition the high reputation he has gained.

By the same author

ONE WORD AND ANOTHER
RIGHT WORD, WRONG WORD
THE CHOICE OF WORDS
A SECOND BOOK OF ENGLISH IDIOMS
THIRD BOOK OF ENGLISH IDIOMS
A BOOK OF ENGLISH PROVERBS

A BOOK OF ENGLISH IDIOMS

by

V. H. COLLINS

LONGMANS

LONGMANS, GREEN AND CO LTD
48 GROSVENOR STREET, LONDON W1
RAILWAY CRESCENT, CROYDON, VICTORIA, AUSTRALIA
443 LOCKHART ROAD, HONG KONG
PRIVATE MAIL BAG 1036, IKEJA (LAGOS)
44 JALAN AMPANG, KUALA LUMPUR
ACCRA, AUCKLAND, IBADAN, KINGSTON (JAMAICA)
NAIROBI, SALISBURY (RHODESIA)
LONGMANS SOUTHERN AFRICA (PTY) LTD
THIBAULT HOUSE, THIBAULT SQUARE, CAPE TOWN
LONGMANS, GREEN AND CO INC
119 WEST 40TH STREET, NEW YORK 18
LONGMANS, GREEN AND CO
137 BOND STREET, TORONTO 2
ORIENT LONGMANS PRIVATE LTD
CALCUTTA, BOMBAY, MADRAS
DELHI, HYDERABAD, DACCA

First published 1956
Second edition 1957
Third edition 1958
New impression (fourth printing) 1961

PRINTED IN GREAT BRITAIN BY
WESTERN PRINTING SERVICES LTD, BRISTOL

TO

GEORGE HENRY VALLINS

Whose linguistic knowledge and acute
and balanced judgment have always
been my constant admiration

CONTENTS

	PAGE
Preface	ix
List of Idioms	1
Idioms	28
Index	249

PREFACE

In compiling a selection of idioms, out of the thousands in the language, the natural course has been to choose those that are today in most frequent use.

This has ruled out a number of expressions that even within living memory were common but are now obsolescent or obsolete, for much in our language, including idioms, is in a constant, though not usually rapid, state of change.

In studying idioms one is confronted, apart from any question of the current meaning of an expression, by two main problems. The first is its origin. As Pearsall Smith has pointed out, there are a number of idiomatic phrases for which even specialists have not been able to find a completely certain explanation. Secondly there may be a problem of the connection between the origin and the current use. It has often been necessary, in dealing with an idiom of which the current meaning is clear and that is generally used correctly, to state that the connection between the origin and the meaning is unknown.

Sometimes a dominating factor in the formation or the popularity of an idiom must have been a desire for euphony, alliteration, rhyme, repetition, etc.: as for example, to take a few of those dealt with in this book, in *bag and baggage*, *at sixes and sevens*, *rack and ruin*, *high and dry*, *by hook or by crook*. Even when the origin of a phrase is unknown, or when the connection between the origin and the current meaning is obscure, the formation of an idiom could seldom have been mere bedevilment, any more than, in usage in general, are the grossest verbal and syntactical misuses. Nevertheless Pearsall Smith, referring to what he calls 'the expressiveness of irrelevant phrases', goes so far as to suggest that this shows a love for the illogical and absurd, a reluctance to submit to reason, which break loose now and then, so that sometimes the human mind seems to prefer irrelevance as appealing to the imagination and adding to a phrase's vividness and charm.

As to exclusions, my usual practice has been to omit idioms where the question at issue is one of grammar, and that belong more properly, not to a book confined to idioms, but to one of a more general and comprehensive sort, such as those by Mr. G. H. Vallins and Mr. Eric Partridge.

Single and compounded words, similes, and proverbs are not often included, nor quotations except when they are of one or more words that, divorced from the rest of a quotation, have come to have an independent life of their own: e.g. 'the green-eyed monster' (*Othello*). Another group that has usually been excluded is that of verbs compounded with prepositions of adverbial force. To have given these even a moderate representation would have increased far beyond the extent contemplated a book that does not aim at being a dictionary. Thus while there does appear a group of idioms dealing with *hang* that contains *hang fire*, *hang by a thread*, *hang on like grim death*, it does not include *hang back*, *hang on*, *hang over*.

A considerable number of colloquialisms have been included, and a few slang phrases. There is often no clear line between slang and colloquialisms, or between either of these and established literary English. Many a word or phrase that some years ago was used chiefly or entirely by the rough and the uneducated, and would have been regarded as slang, becomes a colloquialism used by the educated, and still later on may become established literary idiom. Dean Alford in *The Queen's English*, published in the second half of last century, referred to the phrase **come to grief** as 'almost a slang phrase or one that has but lately ceased to be one'. It is many years since then that the phrase has become established and dignified literary idiom. H. W. Fowler, who is regarded by many as a pedant of pedants, said that 'the idiomatic speaker and writer differs chiefly from the slangy in using what was slang and is now idiom'.

Phrases, and, when rarely they are given, single and compounded words, that, it is thought, would be regarded by most educated people as slang have been marked by (S).

In standard spoken and written English today idiom is an established, universal and essential element that, used with care, ornaments and enriches the language. This was not always recognised. Pearsall Smith in *Words and Idioms*, published nearly thirty years ago, mentions what was thought of idioms in the eighteenth century. They were then regarded as vulgarisms and offences against logic and reason. Addison used them in his prose, but thought they ought not to be used in poetry. Dr. Johnson wished to abolish them. He declared that in his dictionary he had tried to clear the language from 'colloquial barbarisms, licentious idioms, and irregular constructions'. Today such opinions as these would be regarded as absurd.

Some writers use idioms more than others. From this point of view one could often divide writers into two classes: those who use them much, and those who use them little. Thus Dickens falls into the first class, Galsworthy into the second. There are dangers on both sides. Contemporary writing that is almost destitute of idioms can give an impression of flatness. On the other hand idioms can be overworked. Their use can reach a degree of frequency that deprives the writing of freshness. They often become clichés.

Naturally a sheet-anchor throughout has been the Oxford Dictionaries. References are generally to the *Concise Oxford Dictionary* and the *Shorter Oxford English Dictionary*, as these books have been at my elbow, though, when necessary, I have consulted and cited the big *Oxford English*

Dictionary. The Delegates of the Clarendon Press have given generous leave for the many references to and quotations from these books.

The following abbreviations have been used:

O.E.D.: The Oxford English Dictionary;

S.O.E.D.: The Shorter Oxford English Dictionary, revised and edited by C. T. Onions, Third Edition, revised with Addenda, 1955;

C.O.D.: The Concise Oxford Dictionary of Current English, by H. W. Fowler and F. G. Fowler, Fourth Edition, revised by E. McIntosh, with Addenda, 1954.

Much information has been gathered from two mines of erudition, *The Oxford Dictionary of English Proverbs*, by W. G. Smith, edited by J. E. Heseltine, revised by Sir Paul Harvey; and Mr. Burton Stevenson's *Book of Proverbs, Maxims and Familiar Phrases*. These contain dated records of the use of proverbs, and sometimes of phrases that marked stages in their development before they became crystallised and established in their present current use. Mr. Stevenson's book especially is rich in records of early use.

Among other sources consulted a special acknowledgment is due to a book, now out of print, from which I have gained much: *Everyday English Phrases* (1937), by Mr. J. S. Whitehead, with its clear definitions, interesting citations, and ingenious conjectures.

OO has been marked against an idiom of which the origin is obscure when the obscurity has not otherwise been mentioned.

I owe warm thanks for help given me by the following, including a number of strangers who placed at my service their authoritative knowledge: Mrs. L. Allen, Rev. W. M. Atkins, Mr. R. A. Auty, Mr. J. Carr, Dr. Sydney J. Cole,* Mr. A. F. Dick, Mrs. P. E. Dowson, Miss C. Dowson, Professor G. R. Driver, Mr. David Evans, Mr. Ernest Gold,

* (who to my deep regret has since died)

Mrs. Nancy Henry, Admiral Sir William James, Miss Rosemary Lacey, Professor E. G. T. Liddell, Mrs. D. Pigott, the Rev. Prebendary J. H. Powell, Mr. C. Matheson, Professor H. J. Rose, Mr. E. Simpson, Mrs. M. Sewell, Mrs. Ann Thomas, Mrs. H. B. Thomas, Professor W. S. Watt, Professor Westrup; and, from first to last, ever patiently ready to be interrupted in whatever she was doing, my wife.

NOTE TO THE SECOND EDITION

THE success of the first impression of this book has given me a gratifying opportunity, much sooner than I had dared to hope, of seeing incorporated in a second edition a number of corrections and revisions. A majority of them have been of small details, but some have been substantial, and a few serious. For the criticisms and suggestions that have led to these I am warmly grateful to friends, to acquaintances, and to strangers who have kindly taken the trouble to write to me. In particular I am indebted to Mr. R. A. Auty, Mr. B. E. Copping, Mr. Raymond Mortimer, and Mr. G. D. H. Pidock.

1956

LIST OF IDIOMS

1 A 1
2 Achilles' heel
3 the acid test
4 in the air
5 all at sea
6 all eyes (for)
7 All his geese are swans
8 All is grist that comes to his mill
9 all my eye (or all in my eye)
10 all over
11 He is all there
12 He is not all there (or not quite all there)
13 in all conscience
14 It is all one
15 It is all square
16 It is all up (or All is up)
17 on all fours
18 put all one's eggs in one basket
19 when all is said and done
20 Anno Domini
21 in apple-pie order
22 the apple of discord
23 the apple of one's eye
24 an April fool
25 as it were
26 asking for it
27 at that
28 an axe to grind
29 a bad egg
30 a bad hat
31 a bad lot
32 bag and baggage

33 have the ball at one's feet
34 Then the balloon went up
35 be on the band-wagon
36 Then the band played
37 His bark is worse than his bite
38 bark up the wrong tree
39 on one's beam-ends
40 bear the palm
41 beard the lion (or a person)
42 beat (or flog) a dead horse
43 beat a person to it
44 beat about the bush
45 beat hollow
46 beat the air
47 a bed of roses
48 have a bee in one's bonnet
49 a bee line
50 beer and skittles
51 beg the question
52 beggar description
53 beside oneself
54 the best of both worlds
55 a big bug
56 bird of passage
57 a bit thick
58 bite a person's head off
59 bite off more than one can chew
60 to the bitter end
61 a black sheep
62 blind side
63 blood and thunder
64 Blood is thicker than water
65 a blot in one's escutcheon (or 'scutcheon)
66 to blot one's copy-book
67 blow hot and cold
68 blow the gaff
69 a blue funk
70 be in (or have) the blues
71 blue ribbon (or riband)

72 once in a blue moon
73 true blue
74 (1) a bolt from the blue; (2) out of the blue
75 a bone of contention
76 a bone to pick
77 bring to book
78 in one's black (or bad) books
79 in one's good books
80 speak by the book
81 suit one's book
82 take a leaf out of a person's book
83 turn over a new leaf
84 The boot is on the other leg
85 be born on the wrong side of the blanket
86 be born with a silver spoon in one's mouth
87 borrowed plumes
88 a bottle-neck
89 brand (or bran) new
90 a bread and butter letter
91 break a butterfly on a wheel
92 break a lance with
93 break new ground
94 break the back
95 break the ice
96 break the neck
97 break the record
98 the breath of one's nostrils
99 bring down the house
100 bring (or drive or strike) home (to one)
101 bring grist to the mill
102 It is as broad as it is long
103 a broken reed
104 a brown study
105 browned off
106 bumbledom
107 burn one's fingers
108 burn one's boats
109 burn the candle at both ends
110 burn the midnight oil

111 bury one's head in the sand
112 bury the hatchet
113 buy a pig in a poke
114 by and large
115 let bygones be bygones
116 a feather in his cap
117 cap in hand
118 The cap fits
119 set one's cap
120 on the carpet
121 carry coals to Newcastle
122 carry on
123 carry one's point
124 in the cart
125 cast (or throw or fling) in a person's teeth
126 cast one's bread upon the waters
127 cast pearls before swine
128 castles in Spain
129 castles in the air
130 catch a Tartar
131 catch at (or clutch) a straw
132 caviare to the general
133 as different as chalk is from cheese
134 by a long chalk
135 chalk it up (against a person)
136 from China to Peru
137 a chip of the old block
138 a clean sweep
139 cleanse the Augean stables
140 a close shave
141 a close thing
142 under a cloud
143 in clover
144 a cock and bull story
145 cock-a-hoop
146 cock of the walk
147 cocksure
148 cocky
149 live like fighting cocks

150 cold comfort
151 have cold feet
152 Colonel Blimp
153 come off with flying colours
154 false colours
155 give (or lend) colour to
156 like to see the colour of his money
157 nail one's colours to the mast
158 off colour
159 paint in bright colours
160 put a false colour on
161 strike one's colours
162 true colours
163 come a cropper
164 come down like a ton of bricks
165 come down on the right side of the fence
166 come (or get) down to brass tacks
167 come down to earth
168 come to grief
169 come to, come to oneself
170 when the cows come home
171 a contradiction in terms
172 count one's chickens before they are hatched
173 crocodile tears
174 cross as two sticks
175 cross swords (or measure swords)
176 cross (or pass) the Rubicon
177 as the crow flies
178 cry stinking fish
179 cudgel one's brains
180 my cup of tea
181 cupboard love
182 in one's cups
183 curry favour
184 a curtain lecture
185 cut a dash
186 cut a figure
187 cut and dried
188 cut and run

189 cut both ways
190 cut it fine
191 cut off one's nose to spite one's face
192 cut off with a shilling
193 cut one's coat according to one's cloth
194 cut one's losses
195 cut out
196 Cut the cackle and come to the horses (or 'osses)
197 cut the Gordian knot
198 cut to the quick
199 cut up rough
200 damn with faint praise
201 a damp squib
202 a Darby and Joan
203 a dark horse
204 The darkest place is under the candlestick
205 any day
206 call it a day
207 day in and day out, or day in, day out
208 for a rainy day
209 His (or Its) days are numbered
210 palmy days
211 pass the time of day
212 seen better days
213 the day (or a day) after the fair
214 dead as a door-nail
215 dead as mutton
216 a dead letter
217 dead men's shoes
218 dead sea fruit
219 die game
220 a die-hard
221 give up the ghost
222 go west
223 hang on like grim death
224 in at the death
225 kick the bucket
226 pass away
227 passing

228 to the death
229 turn up one's toes
230 the deepest dye
231 out of one's depth
232 between the devil and the deep sea
233 play the devil (or deuce) with
234 the devil to pay
235 to give the devil his due
236 the Dickens
237 do in Rome as the Romans do
238 a dog in the manger
239 a dog's life
240 Dog does not eat dog
241 dog-tired
242 go to the dogs
243 Let sleeping dogs lie
244 a cat and dog life
245 a cat's-paw
246 get (or put) a person's back up
247 let the cat out of the bag
248 not room to swing a cat
249 rain cats and dogs
250 rub a person up the wrong way
251 see how the cat jumps
252 sick as a cat; sick as a dog
253 in the doldrums
254 donkey-work
255 donkey's years
256 dot one's i's and cross one's t's
257 down and out
258 down at heel
259 down in the mouth
260 draw a bow at a venture
261 draw the long bow
262 Draw it mild
263 dressed up to the nines
264 drink like a fish
265 drop a brick
266 a drug on the market

267 not so dusty
268 Dutch courage
269 on earth
270 Dog does not eat dog
271 eat humble pie
272 eat one's cake and have it
273 eat one's heart out
274 eat one's words
275 The proof of the pudding is in the eating
276 elbow grease
277 out at elbow(s)
278 at the eleventh hour
279 at a loose end
280 burn the candle at both ends
281 end in smoke
282 go off the deep end
283 make ends (or both ends) meet
284 make one's hair stand on end
285 on one's beam-ends
286 the end of one's tether
287 the fag-end
288 the thin end of the wedge
289 the wrong end of the stick
290 to the bitter end
291 enough rope
292 all my eye (or all in my eye)
293 cast sheep's eyes
294 see eye to eye
295 the apple of one's eye
296 The scales fell from his eyes
297 throw dust in a person's eyes
298 up to the eyes
299 with half an eye
300 with one's eyes open
301 cut off one's nose to spite one's face
302 fly in the face of
303 have the face
304 in the face of
305 keep a straight face

306 laugh on the wrong side of his mouth (or other side of his face)
307 lose face
308 on the face of it
309 pull (or draw or wear) a long face
310 put a bold face on
311 put a good face on
312 save one's face
313 set one's face against
314 show one's face
315 throw in a person's face
316 face about
317 face it out
318 face the music
319 face up to
320 two-faced; double-faced
321 the fag-end
322 is (or sounds or reads) like a fairy tale
323 fall between two stools
324 fall foul of
325 fall on one's feet
326 The scales fell from his eyes
327 a far cry from
328 The fat was in the fire
329 birds of a feather
330 a feather in his cap
331 feather one's nest
332 Fine feathers make fine birds
333 in fine (or good or grand or full or high) feather
334 ruffle a person's feathers
335 show the white feather
336 smooth one's rumpled feathers
337 fed up
338 feel in one's bones
339 fifty-fifty
340 fight shy
341 fight with one's back to the wall
342 burn one's fingers
343 have a finger in the pie

344 slip through one's fingers
345 snap one's fingers
346 at the first blush
347 a fish out of water
348 a kettle of fish
349 neither fish, flesh, fowl, nor good red herring
350 other fish to fry
351 to cry stinking fish
352 to drink like a fish
353 to fish in troubled waters
354 a flash in the pan
355 That's flat (or And that's flat)
356 a flea in his ear
357 a flea-bite
358 flesh is heir to
359 flutter the dovecotes
360 the fly in the ointment
361 a fool's errand
362 fall on one's feet
363 have cold feet
364 have the ball at one's feet
365 not let the grass grow under one's feet
366 put one's foot down
367 put one's foot in it
368 set on foot
369 shake the dust from one's feet
370 stand on one's own feet (or legs)
371 step off on the wrong foot
372 foot the bill
373 a forlorn hope
374 forty winks
375 free lance
376 friend at court
377 That is his (or her or their) funeral
378 gall and wormwood
379 a game leg
380 scratch team, crew, etc.
381 play fair
382 play a person false

383 play the game
384 The die is cast
385 The game is not worth the candle
386 The game is up
387 within an ace
388 above (or open and above) board
389 call a man's bluff
390 a clean sweep
391 to follow suit
392 have a card up one's sleeve
393 a house of cards
394 is on the cards
395 leave in the lurch
396 pass the buck to
397 play fast and loose
398 play one's cards well
399 put one's cards on the table
400 show one's hand
401 sweep the board
402 throw in one's hand
403 turn the tables
404 a trump
405 a trump card
406 play your last trump
407 trump up
408 turn up trumps
409 below the belt
410 (1) come up, (2) bring up, to scratch
411 play for safety
412 There's the rub
413 from pillar to post
414 have the ball at one's feet
415 keep the ball rolling
416 knuckle under; knuckle down
417 on one's toes
418 toe the line; toe the mark
419 a gay Lothario
420 get (or put) a person's back up
421 get cracking

422 get down to bedrock
423 get it in the neck
424 get no change out of a person
425 get one's goat
426 get one's monkey up
427 get the hang of
428 got out of bed on the wrong side
429 (1) get, (2) have, the wind up
430 get wind of
431 gild the pill
432 gird (or gird up) one's loins
433 give a handle
434 give a leg up
435 give a person the cold shoulder
436 give a wide berth to
437 give chapter and verse
438 to give the devil his due
439 go at it hammer and tongs
440 go back on
441 go by the board
442 go off the deep end
443 go one better
444 go out of one's way
445 go over the ground
446 go the whole hog
447 go through fire and water
448 go through thick and thin
449 go to one's head
450 go to pot
451 go to the dogs
452 go to the wall
453 go west
454 goes without saying
455 touch and go
456 in one's good books
457 put a good face on
458 throw good money after bad
459 against the grain
460 grasp the nettle

461 a grass widow
462 the Greek Kalends
463 the green-eyed monster
464 up a gum-tree
465 by (or within) a hair's breadth (or hairbreadth)
466 make one's hair stand on end
467 not turn a hair
468 to a hair
469 to split hairs
470 cap in hand
471 from hand to mouth
472 hand in (or and) glove
473 have the whip hand
474 put one's hand to the plough
475 show one's hand
476 wash one's hands
477 get the hang of
478 hang by a thread
479 hang fire
480 hang on by one's eyelids (or eyelashes or eyebrows)
481 hang in the balance
482 hang in the wind
483 hang on like grim death
484 hard and fast
485 has had it
486 the hat trick
487 haul over the coals
488 haul up
489 bite a person's head off
490 bury one's head in the sand
491 go to one's head
492 head over ears
493 Heads I win, tails you lose
494 heap coals of fire on a person's head
495 hit the nail (or the right nail) on the head
496 It is on your (or your own) head; On your head be it
497 keep one's head
498 keep one's head above water
499 lose one's head

500 make head or tail of it
501 off one's head
502 put one's head in the lion's mouth
503 run one's head against a stone wall
504 talk a person's head off
505 turn one's head
506 heal the breach
507 have one's heart in one's boots
508 have one's heart in one's mouth
509 He has his heart in the right place
510 warm the cockles of one's heart
511 wear one's heart on one's sleeve
512 hide one's light under a bushel
513 highfaluting (or highfalutin)
514 hit it off
515 hit off
516 Hobson's choice
517 hocus-pocus
518 hoist with his own petard
519 to hold the baby
520 hold water
521 hole and corner
522 by hook or by crook
523 the ins and outs
524 the iron had entered into his soul
525 irons in the fire
526 a Job's comforter
527 jump from the frying-pan into the fire
528 It's just one of those things
529 keep a stiff upper lip
530 keep one's head
531 keep one's head above water
532 keep one's (or another's) nose down to the grindstone
533 to keep the pot boiling
534 a kettle of fish
535 kick one's heels
536 kick over the traces
537 kill the goose that lays the golden eggs
538 kill two birds with one stone

539 a King Charles's head
540 knock into a cocked hat
541 I do not know him from Adam
542 know all the answers
543 know on which side one's bread is buttered
544 know the ropes
545 on its last legs
546 the last straw
547 laugh in (or up) one's sleeve
548 laugh on the wrong side of his mouth (or on the other side of his face)
549 (1) lay at a person's door; (2) lie at a person's door
550 lead a person up the garden (or garden path)
551 Least said, soonest mended
552 leave a person flat
553 leave no stone unturned
554 a left-handed compliment
555 Let (or Leave) well alone
556 lick into shape
557 If you don't like it, you can lump it
558 one's line of country
559 a lion in the path
560 beard the lion
561 put one's head into the lion's mouth
562 the lion's share
563 A little bird told me
564 lock, stock, and barrel
565 lock the stable door after the horse is stolen
566 the long arm of coincidence
567 in the long run
568 look a gift-horse in the mouth
569 at a loose end
570 What one loses on the swings one gains on the roundabouts
571 (1) to lose (or break) the thread; (2) to pick up the threads
572 to be down on one's luck
573 mad as a hatter
574 mad as a March hare
575 make a virtue of necessity
576 make anything of it

577 make bricks without straw
578 make ends (or both ends) meet
579 make hay of
580 make hay while the sun shines
581 make head or tail of it
582 make it
583 make mincemeat (of)
584 make no bones
585 make one's gorge rise
586 make one's hair stand on end
587 make rings round a person
588 the man in the street
589 mealy-mouthed
590 barmy (or balmy)
591 batty (or bats)
592 dotty
593 gaga
594 half-baked
595 have a screw loose
596 have a slate missing (or loose)
597 He is not all (or not quite all) there
598 midsummer madness
599 off one's head
600 potty
601 scatty
602 screwy
603 soft
604 have a tile missing (or loose)
605 mince matters
606 mind (or be on) one's P's and Q's
607 miss the bus
608 a month of Sundays
609 More power to your elbow
610 Mrs. Grundy
611 nail to the counter
612 namby-pamby
613 a near miss
614 a near (or close) shave
615 a near (or close) thing

616 break the neck
617 get it in the neck
618 neck and crop
619 neck and neck
620 neck or nothing
621 a nest-egg
622 nigger in the wood-pile
623 cut off one's nose to spite one's face
624 keep one's (or another's) nose down to the grindstone
625 led by the nose
626 pay through the nose
627 put a person's nose out of joint
628 Nosey Parker
629 not a leg to stand on
630 not a patch on
631 not fit to hold a candle to
632 not let the grass grow under one's feet
633 not room to swing a cat
634 not to be sneezed (or sniffed) at
635 One cannot see the wood for the trees
636 One cannot make a silk purse out of a sow's ear
637 One cannot put the clock back
638 be nuts on
639 for nuts
640 O.K.
641 odour of sanctity
642 out-Herod Herod
643 paddle one's own canoe
644 be at pains; take pains
645 for one's pains
646 on (or under) pain
647 pains and penalties
648 paint the lily
649 beyond the pale
650 palm off
651 palmy days
652 a Parthian shot (or shaft)
653 pass the time of day
654 patience on a monument

655 a Paul Pry
656 pay (or pay back) in his own coin
657 pay on the nail
658 pay a person out
659 pay the piper
660 pay through the nose
661 the devil to pay
662 peter out
663 to pick up the threads
664 at a pinch
665 in the pink
666 the pipe of peace
667 the piping times of peace
668 as plain as a pikestaff
669 have too much on one's plate
670 play ducks and drakes
671 play second fiddle
672 play the devil (or deuce) with
673 play to the gallery
674 play up to
675 IDIOMS FROM GAMES
676 plough the sands
677 a pot (usually a big pot)
678 go to pot
679 keep the pot boiling
680 take pot luck
681 the pot calling the kettle black
682 a pound of flesh
683 pour oil on troubled waters
684 the powers that be
685 a pretty pickle
686 only pretty Fanny's way
687 prick up one's ears
688 the primrose path
689 The proof of the pudding is in the eating
690 the psychological moment
691 pull a person's leg
692 pull one's weight
693 (1) pull strings; (2) pull the strings

694 pull the chestnuts out of the fire
695 put a false colour on
696 put (or get) a person's back up
697 put a person's nose out of joint
698 put a spoke in a person's wheel
699 put all one's eggs in one basket
700 put on the slate (against a person)
701 put on side
702 put on the screw
703 put one's foot down
704 put one's foot in it
705 put one's hand to the plough
706 put one's head in the lion's mouth
707 put (or lay or set) one's shoulder to the wheel
708 Put that in your pipe and smoke it
709 put the cart before the horse
710 put the lid on it
711 put two and two together
712 stay put
713 a Pyrrhic victory
714 queer a person's pitch
715 in Queer Street
716 on the Q T (or q t)
717 rack and ruin
718 for a rainy day
719 It never (or seldom) rains but it pours
720 raise Cain
721 raise the wind
722 a raw deal
723 read between the lines
724 red herring
725 like a red rag to a bull
726 red tape
727 see red
728 rest on one's laurels; rest on one's oars
729 ride the high horse
730 ride for a fall
731 ride hell for leather
732 ride roughshod over

733 ring a bell
734 rob Peter to pay Paul
735 a Roland for an Oliver
736 a rolling stone
737 rope in
738 a rough diamond
739 a round robin
740 round-table conference
741 rub in
742 by rule of thumb
743 rule the roost
744 a run for one's money
745 cut and run
746 in the long run
747 run amuck (or amok)
748 run one's head against a stone wall
749 run riot
750 run the gauntlet
751 run to earth
752 The sands are running out
753 S O S
754 in sackcloth and ashes
755 sail close to the wind
756 the salt of the earth
757 in the same boat
758 in the same box
759 by the same token
760 tarred with the same brush
761 The sands are running out
762 Satan rebuking sin
763 save the mark
764 goes without saying
765 Least said, soonest mended
766 He cannot say (or cry) Bo to a goose
767 Says you
768 What he says goes
769 when all is said and done
770 The scales fell from his eyes
771 in a scrape

772 scot free
773 scotch the snake
774 between Scylla and Charybdis
775 One cannot see the wood for the trees
776 See how the cat jumps
777 See how the land lies
778 See how the wind blows
779 see red
780 seen better days
781 sell the pass
782 send to Coventry
783 separate the sheep from the goats
784 set a stone rolling
785 set by the ears
786 set on foot
787 set one's teeth on edge
788 set the Thames on fire
789 Sez (or Says) you
790 shake the dust from one's feet
791 no great shakes
792 Shanks's mare
793 sheet-anchor
794 on the shelf
795 dead men's shoes
796 in a person's shoes
797 on a shoe-string
798 That is another pair of shoes
799 where the shoe pinches
800 shoot one's bolt
801 short-circuit
802 short shrift
803 show-down
804 show one's face
805 show one's hand
806 show one's teeth
807 show the cloven hoof
808 shut (or slam) the door
809 sign on the dotted line
810 sing a different tune

811 sink or swim
812 a Sisyphean task
813 sit on the fence
814 It is six of one to half a dozen of the other
815 at sixes and sevens
816 skate on thin ice
817 a skeleton in the cupboard
818 slap-dash (or slapdash or slap dash)
819 sleep like a top
820 sleep on the matter
821 slip through one's fingers
822 small beer
823 small fry
824 the small hours
825 There's no smoke without fire
826 a snake in the grass
827 snap one's fingers
828 So long!
829 up to snuff
830 soft soap
831 sold a pup
832 something in the wind
833 for a song
834 a sop to Cerberus
835 sound as a bell
836 sounding brass
837 in the soup
838 sour grapes
839 sow one's wild oats
840 sow the wind and reap the whirlwind
841 speak by the card
842 speak with (or have) one's tongue in one's cheek
843 spick and span (or spick and span new)
844 spike a person's guns
845 split hairs
846 split the difference
847 spoil the Egyptians
848 spoil the ship for a ha'porth of tar
849 sponge on

850 a sprat to catch a mackerel
851 up the spout
852 spread like wildfire
853 be on the square
854 a round peg in a square hole (or a square peg in a round hole)
855 a square (or fair and square) deal
856 a square meal
857 four square
858 get a matter square
859 It is all square
860 We will call it square
861 hit square (or squarely)
862 play square (or squarely)
863 square a person
864 square an account
865 square accounts
866 to square the circle
867 square up
868 square with
869 make one's hair stand on end
870 not a leg to stand on
871 stand in a person's light
872 stand on one's own feet (or legs)
873 stand in a white sheet
874 His star was in the ascendant
875 stay put
876 steal a march on
877 steal a person's thunder
878 out of step
879 step off on the wrong foot
880 stew in his own juice
881 stick to one's guns
882 to stomach
883 a storm in a teacup
884 straight from the horse's mouth
885 straight from the shoulder
886 a straight tip
887 strain at a gnat

888 up my street
889 streets ahead
890 stretch (or strain) a point
891 strike oil
892 Strike while the iron is hot
893 That's the stuff to give him (her, them)
894 *sub rosa*
895 swan song
896 swing the lead
897 the sword of Damocles
898 to a T
899 take a person down a peg
900 take French leave
901 take in one's stride
902 take off one's hat to
903 take pot luck
904 take the bit between one's teeth
905 take the bull by the horns
906 take the gilt off the gingerbread
907 take (or carry) the can
908 take the cake (or biscuit)
909 take the shine out of
910 take time by the forelock
911 take to task
912 take the wind out of a person's sails
913 take with a grain of salt
914 talk a person's head off
915 talk nineteen to the dozen
916 talk shop
917 talk through his hat
918 tarred with the same brush
919 by the skin of his teeth
920 cast (or throw or fling) in a person's teeth
921 get one's teeth into
922 in the teeth of
923 set one's teeth on edge
924 show one's teeth
925 take the bit between one's teeth
926 tooth and nail

927 A little bird told me
928 tell (a person) flat
929 tell a person off
930 tell tales out of school
931 Tell that to the marines
932 You are telling me
933 temper the wind to the shorn lamb
934 on tenterhooks
935 thank one's stars (or one's lucky stars)
936 the thin end of the wedge
937 a thorn in the flesh
938 throw a spanner in the works
939 throw down the gauntlet
940 throw dust in a person's eyes
941 throw good money after bad
942 throw her bonnet (or cap) over the windmill
943 throw (or cast or fling) in a person's teeth
944 throw to the wolves
945 throw up the sponge
946 thrust down a person's throat
947 under the thumb of
948 tick a person off
949 That's the ticket
950 time out of mind
951 times out of (or without) number
952 on tiptoe
953 tit for tat
954 Tom, Dick, and Harry
955 Tommy Atkins; Tommy
956 tommy rot (or tommyrot)
957 from the top drawer
958 topsy-turvy
959 a touch of the tar-brush
960 in touch
961 touch and go
962 trail one's coat
963 tread on a person's corns
964 Even a worm will turn
965 not turn a hair

966 turn a deaf ear
967 turn down
968 turn one's head
969 turn over a new leaf
970 turn the tables
971 turn up trumps
972 twiddle one's thumbs
973 two bites of (or at) a cherry
974 two strings (or a second string) to one's bow
975 That is up to him
976 on one's uppers
977 upset the (or a person's) applecart
978 Use your loaf
979 with a vengeance
980 warm the cockles of one's heart
981 wash one's dirty linen in public
982 be on the water wagon
983 wear one's heart on one's sleeve
984 under the weather
985 a wet blanket
986 wheels within wheels
987 a white elephant
988 a whited sepulchre
989 a wild goose chase
990 win hands down
991 win his spurs
992 get (or have) the wind up
993 get wind of
994 raise the wind
995 sail close to the wind
996 see how the wind blows
997 something in the wind
998 sow the wind and reap the whirlwind
999 temper the wind to the shorn lamb
1000 wipe the floor
1001 cry wolf
1002 keep the wolf from the door
1003 take the wolf by the ears
1004 throw to the wolves

1005 a wolf in sheep's clothing
1006 to wolf
1007 wool-gathering
1008 Even a worm will turn
1009 not to be worth; not to care
1010 not worth his salt
1011 wring one's withers
1012 the writing on the wall
1013 the wrong end of the stick
1014 to be on the wrong tack
1015 You can whistle for (it or that)

1

A 1. *excellent, best, of highest quality, first rate:* 'A', as the first letter of the alphabet, with '1', as the first number, was used to denote a first-class ship in Lloyd's Register; and so came to be used adjectivally, in a general sense, for 'excellent', etc.

2

Achilles' heel. *the one weak spot in a man's circumstances or character.* Anatomists call the great tendon connecting the heel with the calf of the leg 'the tendon of Achilles'. According to legend, Thetis, the mother of Achilles, tried to make her son invulnerable by dipping him in the river Styx, and succeeded except that the heel by which she held him, not being immersed, remained vulnerable. In the Trojan War, Achilles was wounded by an arrow in this spot by Paris, and died of the wound.

To 'bruise the heel of Achilles' is to attack a person or a nation at the weakest point.

3

the acid test. *a decisive, critical, crucial test.* The phrase in its original and scientific sense meant the testing of a substance, to find whether it contained gold, with nitric acid. It then came to be used figuratively in a general sense for subjecting anything to a severe test. At best it is a cliché. Sir Alan Herbert gives an absurd example of its use in an advertisement of flats, where all it meant was that, as he puts it, you may go and have a look at the flats, and by inspection satisfy yourself that they are genuine flats, and not bathing machines or hen-roosts cunningly devised.

4

in the air. These words are often preceded by 'all' or 'quite'. *uncertain.* The phrase is used figuratively with reference to projects, etc. 'Our holiday plans are still in the air.' As the air is virtually omnipresent, to be in the air means being without fixed situation, and so, in an extended sense, without concrete existence. Compare 'vanish into thin air' = 'disappear'.

In another sense the expression is used to mean *much talked about*, with reference to something that has not yet come into existence. 'Federation is in the air.'

5

all at sea. *unable to understand; in a state of ignorance* or *bewilderment about circumstances, a situation, etc.* The metaphor is that of a boat tossed about, out of control, adrift, with its occupant or occupants not knowing where they are.

6

all eyes (for). *with looks concentrated (on).*

7

All his geese are swans. *Ordinary people and things and events he has to do with he regards as remarkable.* The goose (at all events when domesticated) is a bird lacking outstanding appearance; the swan (at all events when in the water) is the most graceful of birds. The phrase is recorded as far back as in Burton's *Anatomy of Melancholy* (1621).

8

All is grist that comes to his mill. 'grist' is corn for grinding. The literal meaning would be that everything that came to his mill was used as corn for grinding. The figurative meaning is that *he succeeds in making profitable use of everything that comes his way.* Compare **bring grist to the mill** (101).

9

all my eye (or **all in my eye**). *nonsense, humbug, a matter for contemptuous disbelief.* The idiom is two centuries old. It may have referred originally to the tears of a person affecting emotion he does not feel: the tears are in his eye, but do not spring from his heart.

There is a later and longer form '**all (in) my eye and Betty Martin**'. The origin of this is unknown. Joe Miller, the eighteenth-century humorist, invented a farcical story that a British sailor, going into a foreign church, heard someone saying, '*O mihi, beate Martine*' meaning 'O grant me aid, blessed St. Martin'; and giving an account of this he said it sounded like '**All my eye and Betty Martin**'.

10

all over. *characteristically.* 'He has never written even to acknowledge the cheque, but that is Bill all over.' 'that is Bill all over' is an elision of 'Bill, all over him ("him" = "his character"), is like that'.

He is all there. This means much more than the opposite of **He is not all there** (see the next article). It not only implies that he is in full possession of his mental faculty but means that *he is more than ordinarily sharp.*

12

He is not all there (or **not quite all there**). *He is not in full possession of his mental faculties.* The normal person is regarded as having these faculties complete; but, since some of them in the given person are lacking, the entity that should make up his completeness is regarded as not all present.

13

in all conscience. 'a form of asseveration' is *C.O.D.'s* description of this expression. Its nearest synonyms are words like *extremely, certainly, indeed.* 'This simple and easy job he took long enough to do in all conscience.' Like most or perhaps all asseverating words it is generally or always superfluous. Compare **with a vengeance** (979) and **at that** (27).

14

It is all one. *It is a matter of indifference; comes to the same thing:* i.e. with reference to two or more given alternatives, possibilities, circumstances, etc., whatever is done, happens, etc., is, as far as the net result to or effect on the person or persons concerned goes, one and the same. (This may seem a long explanation of two simple words, but many short idioms are closely packed with meaning.)

15

It is all square. *It has been arranged so as to be fair to all sides.*

16

It is all up (or **All is up**). *Everything is at an end; All hope is gone; The situation is hopeless.* The use of 'up' here is strange. One might rather expect, when everything has come to an disastrous end, the word 'down'; but compare **The game is up** (386).

17

on all fours. The conduct of a person that is consistent and uniform. The metaphor is that of a four-legged animal all of whose body as it touches the ground is on the same level.

18

put all one's eggs in one basket. *risk everything* (e.g. money) *in one venture; stake all one's hopes on one source or means.* The phrase is generally used in a warning not to do this, because injury befalling the basket may ruin one entirely.

19

when all is said and done. *when all the facts have been considered; when all the arguments, etc., have been discussed and ended.* 'done' = 'done with'.

20

Anno Domini. *old age. Anno Domini* is Latin for 'In the year of our Lord': i.e. in the year since the birth of Jesus Christ, and, abbreviated to A.D., is used to distinguish a given date in the Christian era from one before that, indicated by B.C. (= Before Christ). As an expression used to refer to the passing of the years in the lifetime of an elderly or old person, it is euphemistic or facetious.

21

in apple-pie order. *perfectly neat or methodical arrange-*

ment. Eliezer Edwards in *Words, Facts, and Phrases* (1884) states that, when the origin of this phrase was discussed in *Notes and Queries*, it was suggested that 'apple-pie' was a corruption of 'alpha, beta' (Greek for '*a, b*'): meaning that an arrangement was as neat as that of the consecutive order of the words of the alphabet. Brewer thinks it was a corruption of the French words *nappe pliée* = 'folded linen sheet'. J. S. Whitehead in *Everyday English Phrases* (1937) suggests that support of this explanation of the origin of the phrase by the term 'apple-pie bed' for the practical joke of folding back, from bottom to top, the under-sheet of a bed, so that on getting into bed a person finds it impossible to stretch his legs further than half-way.

But are not these rather strained efforts to explain a phrase that seems to lend itself to a simple explanation? A good cook tells me that, for an apple pie to look, as well as taste, well, the apples must be carefully cut and arranged and packed in the pie-dish.

22

the apple of discord. *cause of contention.* The allusion is to the apple that the goddess Eris (Discord) threw among the gods and goddesses at the marriage of Thetis and Peleus, to which she had not been invited, and that Paris gave to Venus as the most beautiful of the three goddesses, from which action resulted indirectly the Trojan War.

23

the apple of one's eye. *something extremely precious to one.* The 'apple' is 'the pupil', as being round like an apple, and regarded as the most sensitive and precious part of the eye. The phrase appears in the Bible: 'Keep me as the apple of the eye, hide me under the shadow of thy wings' (*Psalms*, 17, 8).

24

an April fool. *a person who on the first day of April is sportively imposed on.* The origin of the phrase is unknown, though Brewer mentions several conjectures, and Eliezer Edwards, in *Words, Facts, and Phrases* (1884), another.

25

as it were. *so to speak* (= 'as if it were').

26

asking for it. *doing what one ought to know will* (*would*) *cause trouble.* In its figurative sense the expression is always used with reference to a person who the speaker considers ought to have been aware that something he said or did was likely or sure to bring about a given undesirable, perhaps even disastrous, result.

27

at that. *also*, *too*, *moreover*, *etc.*, and sometimes *yet.* 'His work on the house was scamped and superficial, and expensive at that.' This is one of the phrases that we might well put on the list of those to be expelled from the language, and be sure it would not be missed.

28

an axe to grind. *a private end to serve.* The phrase is based on a story told by Benjamin Franklin (1706–90) of how, when he was a boy, a man praised a grindstone in his father's yard; asked him to show how it worked; and, as Franklin turned the wheel, sharpened on it an axe of his own.

Each of the three following phrases has the meaning of a *rascal*, a *scoundrel*, a *worthless person.*

29

a bad egg. *an unsound, unreliable, person or thing*. The phrase came from U.S.A. a century ago. Perhaps an egg was taken as a symbol because it shows in appearance no sign of rottenness but smells offensively. 'Good egg!' is also an exclamatory colloquialism for a welcome piece of news.

30

a bad hat. This expression came into use about 1880. Perhaps a hat has been taken as a symbol here because it is a garment that outwardly covers and hides the head, regarded, in its brain, as the seat of a person's (bad) mind and character.

31

a bad lot. This in its origin is an auctioneering phrase.

32

bag and baggage. *with all one's portable belongings*. The phrase originated in *As You Like It* (III, ii). It is generally used with reference to forced and perhaps ignominious departure. Pearsall Smith in *Words and Idioms* says that it is difficult to find any idioms derived from nineteenth-century writers, and that what he says of that century applies to the present one. 'It is possible to invent a new word', he writes (and he might have added, an extension of meaning of an old word); 'it is possible to write a line of poetry which will go to increase the stock of English quotations; but to add a new idiom to the language seems almost to require powers such as were only possessed by Shakespeare—by Shakespeare, and by thousands of illiterate men and women whose names will never be known.' *bag and baggage* is therefore remarkable, if, as is generally supposed, it originated in a famous speech of Gladstone's about the Turks clearing 'bag and baggage' out of a European province.

This, however, in any case is only half of the story of the phrase. Why, it may be wondered, did Gladstone use a phrase in which the two nouns mean the same? It is an example of a large number of phrasal collocations in the language in which two words are used together for the sake of emphasis, helped moreover, as is not rare, by alliteration. Pearsall Smith mentions about eighty of such phrases: e.g. 'leaps and bounds', 'null and void', 'over and above', 'pick and choose', 'ways and means'; and, showing alliteration, 'might and main', 'rack and ruin'.

33

have the ball at one's feet. *be in circumstances where one should be able to make a success.* The metaphor is no doubt from football: perhaps with reference to a player who is so placed that he can make a shot with a ball at the goal.

34

Then the balloon went up. *This caused great* (usually *unpleasant*) *excitement.* Naturally in an age of aeroplanes this idiom is not used as much as it was when a balloon ascent would be a highly sensational popular spectacle.

35

be on the band-wagon. *be able effectively to influence affairs.* The reference is usually to political affairs. The person on a band-wagon can decide on the tunes, and interfere with the playing of them. There is also the phrase 'climb onto the band-wagon' = 'join the victorious party'. (S) from U.S.A.

36

Then the band played. (S) *Then there were excited expressions of dissent*, etc.; or even *Then there was a row.* On the stage, in light variety performances, at the climax of an episode, etc., the band may strike up.

37

His bark is worse than his bite. *What he does is not so bad or serious as what his words seem to threaten.* The metaphor is that of a dog who barks fiercely but does not bite one.

38

bark up the wrong tree. *denounce the wrong person or thing.* The phrase may allude to a dog barking at a cat that has climbed into another tree than the one the dog is barking under.

39

on one's beam-ends. *in a dangerous, especially monetary, state.* This is a nautical idiom. The beams of a ship are the cross-timbers supporting the deck and joining the sides. For the ship to be on her beam-ends means to be tilted so far over on her side that she is in grave danger of sinking.

40

bear the palm. *be the winner; be the best; be pre-eminent:* an allusion to the ancient Romans among whom a branch of the palm tree or a garland of palm leaves was a symbol of victory.

41

beard the lion (or **a person**). *resolutely approach a person, especially a superior, with a demand.* The origin of the use of the verb 'to beard' with the meaning of 'defy', 'openly oppose', is obscure. *S.O.E.D.* only says rather enigmatically 'partly from the idea of taking a lion by the beard'. See 1 *Samuel*, 17 : 34–35: 'There came a lion . . . and . . . I caught him by his beard, and . . . slew him'. A full phrase has 'in his den' added. See Scott's *Marmion*, vi, 14:

And darest thou then
To beard the lion in his den,
The Douglas in his hall?

42

beat (or **flog**) **a dead horse.** *pursue an argument* (especially a destructive one) *when the matter is settled and there is nothing more to discuss.* The allusion seems to be to a person who, when his horse falls down, continues to beat it, not realising it is dead and that nothing more is to be got out of it.

43

beat a person to it. (S) *do it before the other person concerned can get the chance*: i.e. 'anticipate' him (in the primary, established, correct sense of that verb: not used as a slovenly vulgarism for 'expect' or 'foresee'). 'beat' seems to mean 'defeat', 'get the better of'; and 'to' to mean 'in a race to'.

44

beat about the bush. *avoid saying openly, frankly, directly, straight out, what one means; approach a matter in a roundabout way.* The allusion is to beating trees and bushes in order to dislodge birds. Thus we find in Robert Gascoigne in the sixteenth century, 'He bet about the bush whyles others caught the birds'.

45

beat hollow. *defeat thoroughly*, or *be utterly superior to.*

Perhaps 'hollow' is a figurative extension of the image of a person giving another such a beating that he has nothing left inside him. *O.E.D.* suggests that there is a play on the use of 'beat' as meaning both 'defeat' and literally 'strike'.

46

beat the air. *expend violent efforts that can have no result.* The person who invented this expression would have regarded the air as an inert substance with no resisting power that could react to pressure. My friend Charles Matheson tells me that, when as a boy he came across the phrase, the picture he imagined was of a blustering knight on horseback, rushing towards his opponent, and brandishing his weapon wildly, though never getting near enough to do him harm. 'But', he adds, 'what had St. Paul in mind nearly two thousand years ago (there were no jousts then), when he said 'So fight I, not as one that beateth the air'? Perhaps gladiatorial fights: see I *Corinthians*, 15, 32.

47

a bed of roses. The phrase, as suggestive of beautiful and sweet-smelling flowers, and warm, sunny weather, is used figuratively to mean a *situation of ease and comfort.* It is generally used negatively: e.g. 'It was by no means a bed of roses'.

48

have a bee in one's bonnet. *have an obsession about something.* Such a state is compared to that of a person in the hair of whose head, under his cap or hat, there is a bee that makes a continual buzzing.

The phrase is found as far back as in the sixteenth century in Nicholas Udall's *Ralph Roister Doister*: 'whoso hath suche bees as your maister in hys head' (there meaning eccentricities). Compare '**bats**' (591).

49

a bee line. literally: *a direct, straight, shortest, line between two places;* figuratively, in conversation, discussion, etc.: *immediate, direct, approach to, or raising of, a point.* A bee was thought (it is now found, erroneously) to fly always in a straight line to the hive. Compare **as the crow flies** (177).

50

beer and skittles. (S) *fun and pleasure.* 'skittles' is a game played with ninepins. The phrase is generally used negatively: e.g. 'It was not all beer and skittles'. (Used as an interjection 'Skittles!' means 'Nonsense!')

51

beg the question. *in a controversy put forward a point that assumes, takes for granted, what is being discussed and argued about.* The expression goes back to the sixteenth century. 'beg', as used in it, has not any ordinary sense of the verb. It is a translation of the Latin word *petitio* in the logical term *petitio principii.*

As Sir Ernest Gowers points out in *ABC of Plain Words,* the phrase is often wrongly taken to mean that a speaker or writer is evading a straight answer to a question, whereas it means to form a conclusion by making an assumption that is as much in need of proof as the conclusion itself.

52

beggar description. *make description impossible.* 'to beggar' is literally 'to reduce to a state in which one has little or no money'. Figuratively, with reference to description in words, to 'beggar' refers to a thing, event, etc., so remarkable, strange, extraordinary, etc., that it reduces one to a state where one cannot find words to describe it adequately. Shakespeare in *Antony and Cleopatra* (II, iii, 202) makes Enobarbus use the expression in describing Cleopatra.

For her own person,
It beggared all description.

53

beside oneself. *raised to a state of extreme excitement* (grief, joy, etc.), or even *out of one's senses.* The metaphor may on first thoughts seem strange, because 'beside' in its primary sense means 'by the side of', 'close to', 'by one's side'; whereas here the idea is rather that of one's emotions and thoughts being stirred, moved from, outside, one's normal self. But at one time 'beside' had a sense, exactly opposite its present sense, and now obsolete, of 'outside', 'out of', 'away from'.

54

the best of both worlds. *the benefits connected with two different (and perhaps opposed) conditions, circumstances, etc.* The reference is generally to an unsuccessful attempt to get, or to the impossibility of getting, these. A special reference in the use of the phrase is to present life on earth and future life in heaven: e.g. to a person who is at once worldly and spiritual in his aspirations and behaviour.

The earliest record of the use of the phrase does not go back further than to Charles Kingsley in *Westward Ho!* (1855).

55

a big bug. (S) *a person of importance.* A synonymous slang expression is **a big pot** (see 677). *S.O.E.D.*, which gives this as originally from U.S.A. towards the end of the eighteenth century, enters it as connected etymologically with, not 'bug' meaning 'insect', but another word 'bug' = 'bogy', which now survives otherwise in 'bugbear'.

56

bird of passage. *person who is at a given place, or in a given country, only temporarily;* or *person who is constantly moving about without a settled home.* The allusion is to migratory birds.

57

a bit thick. (S) *going too far, outrageous:* i.e. overstepping the bounds of moderation in what one does or says, especially in what one demands. Perhaps the metaphor comes from cutting meat or bread so thick that it cannot be easily eaten, or putting too much butter, etc., on it.

58

bite a person's head off. *speak angrily to a person about something without listening to an explanation or allowing excuses.* The *Oxford Book of English Proverbs* does not give this expression, but it records 'bite a man's nose off' by Thomas Nashe in 1599, and 'snap'd my nose off' by Susanna Centlivre in 1709.

59

bite off more than one can chew. *undertake more than one is able to perform.* The phrase, from U.S.A., is an allusion to the chewing of tobacco.

60

to the bitter end. *to the extreme end, whatever may happen.* Pearsall Smith mentions this among idioms of whose origin 'even specialists have not been able to find a completely certain explanation'.

Eliezer Edwards in *Word, Facts, and Phrases* (1884), who says that the phrase became popular in the American Civil

War, suggests that it is an echo of *Proverbs* 5, 4: 'But her end is bitter as wormwood'. A simple conjecture is that it refers to the bitter dregs of a salutary medicine. I am indebted to Admiral Sir William James for the suggestion that 'bitter' is a corruption of 'better', in a phrase that has a nautical origin, and referred to the days of rope cables of which the outer end became worn by rocks, constant working round capstan, etc., and it became necessary to veer out the cable 'to the better end'.

61

a black sheep. *the one worthless member—the bad lot—of a family, or, sometimes, of a group of people;* or, in a still more general application, *a worthless person.* A flock of sheep sometimes includes one with a black fleece. From this comes the sense in the figurative phrase that the person concerned is an exception. The idea of his being worthless may be connected with the fact that a sheep with black fleece is less valuable than those with white fleeces; but perhaps it may come from a sort of play on the word 'black', which is often used in the sense of morally bad: e.g. 'a black crime', 'a black record', 'black ingratitude'.

62

blind side. *weak part of a person's character that makes him incapable of recognising a fact, a truth, etc.;* or *makes him susceptible to flattery, easily imposed on, etc.* When it comes to these things he is unable to recognise realities.

63

blood and thunder. (noun) *wild melodrama,* (adjective) *wildly melodramatic:* with reference to plays, novels, etc., that have as their stock-in-trade murders and effects intended to be like thunder terrifying.

64

Blood is thicker than water. *The bond created by blood-relationship is stronger than that created by other circumstances:* marriage, friendship, business relations, etc. The connection between the words in the phrase and its current meaning is obscure. There is a well-known anecdote that is sometimes thought to give the origin of the expression, of an American naval officer who in 1859 finding the English in difficulties with the Chinese went to their help, and in his dispatch to his Government justified his interference by using these words. But Stevenson cites Lydgate (1412) for the idea, and the phrase appears in John Ray's *English Proverbs* (1670).

65

a blot in one's escutcheon (or 'scutcheon). *a stain on one's reputation.* An 'escutcheon' is a shield with a person's armorial bearings. This phrase is now rather old-fashioned.

66

to blot one's copy-book. *to commit an indiscretion.* The expression could refer, for example, to conduct in one's profession or business that might injuriously affect one's career. It is generally applied to the masculine sex, and implies on the part of the person deprecating the action disapproval rather than stern condemnation. To 'blot' here means to smudge with ink. A 'copy-book' is an exercise book in which children learn to write.

67

blow hot and cold. *first praise, then blame, a person or thing.* The allusion is to a fable of a satyr who was angry with a visitor for first blowing on his fingers to warm them, and then on his porridge to cool it.

68

blow the gaff. (S) *let out a secret or reveal a plot.* The noun 'gaff' has several meanings, but their connection with this phrase is obscure.

69

a blue funk. (S) *extreme or uncontrollable fear.* People can literally turn a bluish tinge from fear, through disturbance of the circulation of the blood.

70

be in (or have) the blues. *be depressed.* In contrast to red and yellow, which are bright and lively, blue is often dull and low in tint. Cf. **blue devils** = depression.

71

blue ribbon (or riband). *highest distinction.* Thus the blue riband of the Atlantic is the distinction gained by the ship making the quickest crossing of the Atlantic. Specifically the blue ribbon is that of the Order of the Garter. A friend suggests that the phrase comes from *cordon bleu* = 'blue ribbon': a distinction in the French *ancien régime* (later used for a good cook).

72

once in a blue moon. *extremely seldom.* That is the sense in which the expression is used; but how frequent or infrequent is a blue moon?

Under some conditions both sun and moon have a deep blue colour. To go no further back than about twenty-five years, the phenomenon was recorded as having been observed in Ireland in 1927; in California in 1934; in Cairo in 1937; at several places in England and Scotland on 26th September, 1950, and on the following days in Denmark, Switzerland, Italy, Malta, Gibraltar; and near Windsor on 15th December, 1951.

The phenomenon happens when there is fine dust in the atmosphere with particles of suitable size. The dust may be from volcanic eruption, as in 1883 after the eruption of Krakatoa; or maybe blown up from the desert, as in Egypt and Algeria and North China; or it may be caused by forest fires, as in September, 1950, when smoke from fires in Alberta drifted across the Atlantic. A blue sun is commoner than a blue moon, partly because the sun is visible as a full disc every day in clear weather, whereas the moon is a nearly full disc for only half the time that it is visible; partly because people are out-of-doors more by day than by night; partly because the fine dust causing the phenomenon is more likely to be blown up during the day.

Mr. E. Gold, to whom I am indebted for this information, suggested, in 1935, that the operative dust particles must be about the same size as the wave-length of light (a fifty-thousandth of an inch), because the theory of the scattering of light by small particles of a size differing from the wave-length of light indicates that the sun seen through dust of such particles would appear red, as it usually does.

Dr. James Paton adds that it may well be that a blue sun or moon is visible every day or night at some place or other on the globe, though there may not be a person at the right place or time to observe it.

73

true blue. This adjectival phrase, meaning literally 'of a true blue colour', is applied to people of unwavering faith and principle. In a special use the term has been applied in political circles to the Tory party. It is now obsolescent. Pearsall Smith says that it came from the times of the Covenanters, who adopted blue as their colour in contradistinction to the royal red, but *S.O.E.D.* states that it was taken as the colour of constancy as far back as 1500 (a century and a half earlier).

74

(1) **a bolt from the blue;** (2) **out of the blue.** (1) *a sudden, unexpected misfortune.* 'a bolt' here is 'a thunderbolt'; 'the blue' is 'the cloudless sky'. (2) *suddenly and unexpectedly* (not necessarily with reference to a misfortune).

75

a bone of contention. *a matter of sharp division between two people or bodies of people.* The allusion is to a bone that dogs fight for.

76

a bone to pick. *a matter of dispute that must be discussed.* The metaphor seems to be that of a person inviting another to share a meal on a small joint of meat, which, to get the flesh from the bone, has to be carefully carved, or, if one imagines the people using their hands, picked. In the figurative application what the two people are concerned with is a complaint, grievance, accusation, that the speaker has against the other. The idiom is not used with reference to a dispute that is grave. Another and simpler explanation is that the phrase is an alternative way of saying 'I have a bone of contention with you' (see the last article).

The earliest recorded use of the expression is in 1565, but there its meaning is defined as 'to do what was done before; or to busy oneself in a needless employment'.

77

bring to book. *call to account; bring to justice; bring to due punishment.* The phrase seems to be based on the idea of an imaginary book in which a person's bad actions are entered. Cf. 82 and 83.

78

in one's black (or bad) books. *in disfavour; seriously disapproved of.* The phrase may have originated in a practice among shopkeepers and merchants of keeping in separate books notes of good customers and bad customers, good debts and bad. It is recorded as far back as 1592, when Robert Greene entitled one of his books *Black Books Messenger*, and writes, 'Ned Browne's villanies are too many to be described in my Blacke Booke'.

Compare the next article.

79

in one's good books. *in high favour; highly approved of:* the exact contrary of 'in one's bad books' (see the last article).

80

speak by the book. *quote precisely from an authoritative statement.* 'by' = 'according to'.

81

suit one's book. *suit one's plans.* The phrase probably comes from betting on horses, in which a bookmaker will not accept a bet that does not 'suit his book'.

82

take a leaf out of a person's book. *follow a person's example.* The actions of the person imitated are conceived as being entered in an account book. Cf. 77 and next article.

83

turn over a new leaf. *change for the better one's previous conduct.* A person is imagined as following a new rule or set of rules, set out in a fresh page of a book of instructions for guiding his conduct, that will lead to reform. The metaphor is found as early as in John Heywood's collection of proverbs published in 1546.

84

The boot is on the other leg. *The true position is*, or *the circumstances are, exactly the reverse.* The allusion is apparently to a person conceived as putting a boot on his left leg that ought to be on his right, or vice versa. A common use of the idiom is with reference to blame, responsibility, etc., that should be ascribed, not to a person or circumstances A but to B. 'You say he ought to have written to thank me, but the boot is on the other leg, for the obligation is on my side, and it is I that am deeply indebted to him.' A variant for 'leg' is 'foot'.

85

be born on the wrong side of the blanket. *illegitimate.* The metaphor seems to have been based on the idea that the material circumstances of the conception of an illegitimate child were not normal but were irregular and surreptitious: outside, and not, as in marriage, inside, a bed with its appurtenances.

86

be born with a silver spoon in one's mouth. *be born in affluent circumstances, and be brought up in luxury.* The image is that of a child who, belonging to a rich family, is fed with a spoon made of silver, instead of one made with baser material. An early record of the phrase is in James

Kelly's *Scottish Proverbs* (1721): 'Every man is no born with a silver spoon in his mouth'; which he explains as meaning 'every man is not born to an estate, but must labour for his support'. Goldsmith in *The Citizen of the World* (1762) has 'One man is born with a silver spoon in his mouth, and another with a wooden ladle'.

87

borrowed plumes. *qualities, virtues, merits, possessed by another, a person boasts to possess himself.* The allusion is to a fable by Aesop, of a jackdaw that dressed itself up in the feathers of a peacock.

88

a bottle-neck. *an obstruction to an even flow,* especially in industrial production. In its earliest figurative use it meant a narrow outlet for traffic. As Sir Ernest Gowers has pointed out in *ABC of Plain Words*, the phrase needs to be handled carefully in order to avoid absurdity: e.g. when in an explanation of a shortage of goods it is stated that a certain circumstance constitutes 'the largest bottle-neck', for the cause of trouble in bottle-necks is their smallness, narrowness.

89

brand (or **bran) new.** *quite new.* One of the old meanings of 'brand' was an iron stamp for burning a mark in. 'brand (or bran) new' is strictly 'new as if it were from the fire, freshly stamped'.

90

a bread and butter letter. *a letter written to thank a host or hostess for hospitality after a visit.* This is now often called 'a Collins' in allusion to the letter Mr. Collins, in *Pride and Prejudice*, wrote to Mr. Bennet.

91

break a butterfly on a wheel. *use unnecessarily elaborate methods in argument etc. to dispose of a small, trivial matter.* To 'break on the wheel' was a medieval procedure for maiming or killing a person on an instrument of torture that revolved with the victim bound to it. Pope has 'Who breaks a butterfly upon a wheel?' ('Epistle to Dr. Arbuthnot', 305). There used to be also the expression 'a fly on the wheel'. Thus De Quincey has (1859) 'To apply any more elaborate sentiments to them would be to break a fly on the wheel'.

92

break a lance with. *enter into a controversy:* i.e. figuratively, a fight or duel, with a redoubtable opponent. The allusion is to knights in the Middle Ages fighting on horseback with lances. Compare **cross swords (175).**

93

break new ground. Literally this means to break up with the spade, plough, etc., ground that has not previously been cultivated. Figuratively the phrase is used with reference to *finding, in the course of commercial development, new sources for extending business;* or, *in making a speech or in writing, introducing fresh matter, arguments, etc.*

94

break the back (of a task on which one is engaged). *accomplish the most important or difficult part* (of it). 'I think we can now consider that we have broken the back of this job.' The original allusion is to the killing of an animal. The back-bone is the largest, hardest, most resistant part of an animal organism.

95

break the ice. *put an end to formality, stiffness, shyness, in one's relations with people.* The expression in its primary literal sense meant to break the frozen surface of a river, lake, etc., for the passage of boats.

96

break the neck. This means the same as **break the back** (see 94), with a similar allusion, because an animal or human being whose neck is broken is killed.

97

break the record. (*a*) *do something that has not been done before*, or (*b*) *not do something that has always been done before.* Examples of (a): when an athlete runs a race in a shorter time, or jumps higher or further, than has been done before; when a river, overflowing its banks, submerges a greater area that it has done before; when there is a longer drought somewhere at a given time of a year than the Meteorological Office has statistics about. Examples of (b): when a clerk who during all his years of service has always arrived punctually at his office on one occasion does not do so; when owing to an accident a peal of bells that has always rung on Christmas eve does not do so; when over a longer period than has been known before there has not been an eruption of a volcano.

C.O.D. gives as a substitute for 'break' the words 'beat' and 'cut'. 'beat' has a common meaning of 'surpass'. 'cut' perhaps came to be used because a 'record' is primarily an account kept in writing; and, when the new event happens, this account is cancelled, destroyed: as it were, 'cut out'.

98

the breath of one's nostrils. *that which to a given person is* *an essential need and interest*, in the same way that breathing air is necessary to retain life. Cf. *Genesis*, **7**, 22: 'All in whose nostrils was the breath of life'.

99

bring down the house. *give a performance that is a brilliant success and evokes great applause.* Literally the phrase would mean that the applause caused the roof to come down. Its origin is theatrical, but today its use is not confined to theatrical performances.

100

bring (or **drive** or **strike**) **home (to one).** *make (one) realise.* There is also **go** or **come home** with the same sense. The allusion is probably 'touch intimately'.

101

bring grist to the mill. *produce money or profit.* 'grist' is corn for grinding. Compare **All is grist that comes to his mill** (8).

102

It is as broad as it is long. *Either alternative will lead to the same result.* Compare **cut both ways** (189).

103

a broken reed. *a person or thing not giving the help needed.* A reed easily bends. In the Bible (*Isaiah*, 36, 6) a reed injures a man by piercing his flesh.

104

a brown study. *a state of mental absorption* in which a person has no part in the conversation etc. round him. 'brown' used to have a meaning 'gloomy'.

105

browned off. *disgusted, disgruntled, depressed, bored, fed-up.* Lieut.-Col. W. M. C. Wall thinks the expression originated in the Indian Army among soldiers painfully scorched by the sun.

106

bumbledom. The stupid officiousness and pomposity of subordinate officials. The term comes from the name of the beadle in Dickens's *Oliver Twist.*

107

burn one's fingers. *suffer loss, or come to harm, by rash meddling in an affair.* The allusion, when the words were first used figuratively, may have been to a person who gets his fingers burnt when being careless in attending to something cooking on a fire, or trying to fan a flame into a blaze; but Mr. Eric Partridge cites the proverb 'Never burn your fingers to snuff another man's candle'.

108

burn one's boats. *take a step that will make impossible retreat from a course, policy, etc.* The allusion is to the action by military leaders of burning the boats in which an army had crossed a river so that the soldiers would know they must conquer or die, as retreat was impossible.

109

burn the candle at both ends. *dangerously exhaust one's energies by overworking in two different directions.* The expression was used as early as 1730, but the first record of its use in its current meaning goes back only a hundred years, when Charles Kingsley in *Two Years Ago* describes a character who 'burnt the candle at both ends' by sitting up till two in the morning and rising again at six. Here perhaps 'the ends' are regarded as the conclusion of one day and the beginning of the next. But I am told that in Shakespeare's time a candle was sometimes formed by a straw bent in the middle and held erect, alight, by a sort of stand; and that at a later period this was used as a metaphor for extravagance.

110

burn the midnight oil. *work, especially studying or writing, until late at night.* This idiom, at one time popular, is now rare when oil lamps are not much used. There was also an expression, now obsolescent, used in literary criticism, with a deprecatory implication, that a book, etc., 'smelt of the lamp', meaning that it showed excessive signs of erudition or elaboration. The phrase has been traced as far back as to one of the critics of Demosthenes (384–322 B.C.).

111

bury one's head in the sand. *avoid facing facts and recognising realities by pretending that they do not exist.* The allusion is to the fable that ostriches, when hunted, thrust their heads into the sand, thinking that, because they cannot see their enemies, they cannot be seen by them.

112

bury the hatchet. *make up a quarrel.* The allusion is to the custom of the Red Indians, on making peace, of ceremoniously burying their war axes (tomahawks).

113

buy a pig in a poke. *buy a thing without examination or knowledge.* Pigs carried to market in a poke (bag) could not be examined till taken out of this.

114

by and large. *on the whole, all things considered, broadly speaking*. The term in its original sense dates back to the days of sailing ships. *C.O.D.* defines it as meaning in that sense 'to the wind and off it'. Admiral Beamish, in a letter to *The Times* in 1953, said that it referred to keeping a ship on a course so that it made good progress even if the wind varied a few degrees. It is only in recent years that it has become common as a synonym of *on the whole*, etc., though *O.E.D.* cites this use as early as 1833.

115

let bygones be bygones. *put out of mind past unpleasantnesses etc.* Carlyle used 'bygones' to mean former conditions preceding a new era, but the usual reference is to private disagreements etc.

116

a feather in his cap. *an honour to him*, or *a compliment*, or *something he can be proud of*. The metaphor comes from a custom among the Red Indians and other peoples of adding a feather to one's headgear for each enemy killed.

117

cap in hand. *humbly*. The phrase is used of a person who approaches another, in humble spirit, to make a request, ask a favour. The image is that of a servant who addresses his master with his cap off.

118

The cap fits. *The remark, statement, charge, applies truly* (to the person in question).

119

set one's cap (i.e. at a man). *make oneself attractive to him.* The metaphor is based on the idea of a woman's putting on an attractive cap. Today caps are not worn by women. In the Victorian age they were worn by elderly women and servants, but in the eighteenth and early nineteenth centuries women of all ages wore indoors what was called a 'mob-cap' ('mob' in this sense is now obsolete), covering their whole head.

120

on the carpet. *reprimanded by one's superior.* This metaphor must have come into existence at a time when only the rooms of the chief people in an office were carpeted.

121

carry coals to Newcastle. *take something to a place where it is so plentiful that it is not wanted;* figuratively, *do something that is absurdly superfluous.* The first use of the phrase is by Fuller in 1650, though 'as common as coals from Newcastle' appears in 1606. The French have *porter de l'eau à la rivière* ('to carry water to the river').*

122

carry on. *continue.* Pearsall Smith says the origin of the idiom may have been the nautical phrase 'carry on without reefing'. The verb is used also colloquially to mean *behave in an excited, obstreperous, way; take on; go on.*

123

carry one's point. *succeed in gaining one's object or having an argument accepted.* The phrase may come from falconry. *S.O.E.D.* gives 'carry' as having been used in falconry with the meaning of 'fly away with the quarry'. But 'carry' has

* Since this was written the metaphor has lost its point, for now coal has to be sent to Newcastle.

in several current phrases a sense of 'success', which goes back to the early seventeenth century, when it was used for gaining a victory for (a measure, one's candidate, etc.): e.g. 'carry all before one', 'carry the day', 'the resolution was carried'. 'point' = 'what one aims at or contends for'

124

in the cart. *in disastrously serious trouble.* The allusion may be to the cart in which criminals used to be taken to Tyburn for execution. Alternatively the allusion may be to a cart in which a criminal, with the cord from the gallows round his neck, was placed, and that was then drawn forward from under his feet, thus leaving him dangling in the air.

125

cast (or **throw** or **fling) in a person's teeth.** *reproach a person for having done something.* The image seems to be that of aiming a missile at the vulnerable feature of a person's mouth. Compare **throw in a person's face** (315).

The first recorded use of the expression is in 1526 in Tyndale's exposition of the New Testament.

126

cast one's bread upon the waters. *be kind and generous, even in distant quarters, without counting on, at all events immediate, gratitude or return.* Bible (*Ecclesiastes*, 11, 1): 'Cast thy bread upon the waters: for thou shalt find it after many days'.

127

cast pearls before swine. *do things for people, or give or offer them things (especially in the sphere of sentiment, affection, the arts), that they are incapable of appreciating.*

The phrase comes from the Sermon on the Mount: 'Give not that which is holy unto the dogs, neither cast ye your pearls before swine, lest they trample them under their feet, and turn again and rend you' (*Matthew*, 7, 6).

128

castles in Spain. This means the same as **castles in the air** (see next article). French also has *château d'Espagne*. Why 'Spain'? Perhaps because Spain was regarded at one time as a romantic country. The expression appears as far back as the thirteenth century in *The Romaunt of the Rose*:

Thou shalt make castle thanne in Spain,
And dream of joie alle but in vayne.

129

castles in the air. *visionary plans for an achievement of desires unlikely to be realised.*

For idioms connected with cats see 244–252.

130

catch a Tartar. *find that the person in question is more formidable, troublesome, tough, than one had expected.* The Tartars were reputed to be savage, ferocious people.

131

catch at (or **clutch**) **a straw.** *when in extreme danger, anxiety, etc., avail oneself of even the slightest chance of rescue from one's difficulties, or gain hope from the slightest sign that may seem favourable.* The allusion is to the saying that a drowning man will catch at a straw.

132

caviare to the general. *a good thing unappreciated by the general public or by the ignorant.* 'caviare', a delicacy from

Eastern Europe, especially Russia, is the roe of the sturgeon, eaten as a relish. The phrase comes from *Hamlet* (II, ii).

133

as different as chalk is from cheese. *utterly different.* Why chalk and cheese should have been taken as typical of things that differ is obscure. Perhaps they were chosen for the alliterative effect, both words beginning with 'ch'.

134

by a long chalk (less frequent **by long chalks**). *by much.* The origin of the phrase was a former practice of scoring points in games by chalk, before pencils were invented or became common.

135

chalk it up (against a person). *attach blame for it* (to a person); *hold it as a reproach* (against a person). It was the practice, even within the memory of middle-aged people now living, for innkeepers and shopkeepers, especially in poor districts, to enter customers' unpaid accounts on a slate or board or wall, with chalk. Compare **by a long chalk** (134).

136

from China to Peru. *from one side of the world to the other.* This is a quotation from Dr. Johnson's *On the Vanity of Human Wishes*: 'Let observation with extended view Survey mankind from China to Peru'.

137

a chip of the old block. *an inheritor of the characteristics of his father:* as a small piece of wood has the qualities of the large block from which it was cut off. It is generally used in a favourable sense.

138

a clean sweep. *an entire doing away with, a clearing away.* The phrase is generally used only figuratively. For 'clean'= 'entire', 'complete', 'perfect', compare 'to sweep clean'.

139

cleanse the Augean stables. *bring about a drastic reform in some* (usually *public*) *evil.* The allusion is to the fifth labour of Hercules, of cleaning in one day the stables of Augeas, King of Elis, which had three thousand oxen whose stalls had not been cleaned for thirty years. Hercules turned two rivers through the stalls.

140

a close shave: see 614.

141

a close thing: see 615.

142

under a cloud. *in disgrace, in disfavour, with injured reputation.* A cloud is used as a symbol of the atmosphere overhanging misfortune etc., as sunshine is used for betokening prosperity. Compare the proverb 'There is a silver lining to every cloud'.

The metaphor is recorded as being used as far back as 1500.

143

in clover. *in a state of great comfort, ease, and luxury.* Cattle greatly enjoy feeding in a field that has been grown with clover.

144

a cock and bull story. *an absurdly incredible tale.* The earliest recorded use of the phrase is in Burton's *Anatomy of Melancholy* (1621): 'Some men's whole delight is . . . to talk of a Cock and Bull over a pot'. The last words in Sterne's *Tristram Shandy* (1767) are as follows. '"Lord" said my mother, "what is all this story about?" "A cock and a bull", said Yorick—"and one of the best of the kind I ever heard".' Brewer considers that of various conjectures of the origin of the phrase the most probable is that it referred to old fables in which cocks, bulls, and other animals discoursed in human language on things in general. Mr. William Freeman mentions a conjecture that it was a corruption of 'a concocted and bully story' ('bully' from the Danish word *bullen* = 'exaggerated'). The French have an expression in which the animal associated with the cock is not a bull but an ass: *faire des coq-à-l'âne*, which means to talk a lot of nonsense. There is also the use of 'bull' or 'Irish bull' (derived perhaps from the Old French *boul* = 'trickery') for an absurd inconsistency unperceived by the speaker.

By one of those coincidences that now and then add pleasing novelty to the language there exists among soldiers and probably others a colloquially obscene expression, 'That's a lot of cock and bull' = 'That's all nonsense'. (I have heard also, with the same meaning, 'That's only a lot of cow-pat'.)

I am indebted to Capt. L. A. Iles for some of the information in this article.

145

cock-a-hoop. (S) *exuberantly elated.* *S.O.E.D.* says that the origin of the explanation is obscure but that it may have meant setting 'the cock on the hoop': turning on the 'cock' (tap), of a barrel of beer or wine, that is on the 'hoop' (circle of wood or metal binding together the staves), so that, Brewer adds in mentioning this explanation, the company may have a drinking bout. Brewer mentions another explanation: that 'hoop' comes from the French *houpe*, the feathered crest of a cock, and that 'cock-a-hoop' came to mean a lively game-cock.

146

cock of the walk. *head, chief, important, person.* 'walk' is a name given to the enclosure in which poultry is allowed to run freely.

147

cocksure. *confident in opinion.* Probably the phrase is connected, not with 'cock' = 'male bird', 'male domestic fowl', but with 'cock' in another sense, of 'tap', and refers to the certainty of the action of this in preventing an escape of liquor.

148

cocky. *with pert self-confidence.* 'cocky' is an allusion to the arrogant strut of a male domestic fowl.

149

live like fighting cocks. *have ample and excellent food* In the days of cock-fighting (made illegal in 1849) the fighting cocks were highly fed to make them more pugnacious and strong.

150

cold comfort. *small, or no, consolation.* 'comfort' in this sense goes much further back than it does in its modern sense of that which is 'comfortable'. 'None else is there gives comfort to my grief' (Drayton, 1563–1631). The sense is preserved in the hymn 'Abide with me':

'When other helpers fail and comforts flee'.

151

have cold feet. *be frightened or nervous.* Fear tends to reduce the circulation of the blood, and so cause cold, especially in the extremities of the body.

152

Colonel Blimp. A character invented by Mr. D. Low, the cartoonist, typical of the die-hard Tory (see 220).

153

come off with flying colours. *emerge from an affair with honour and great success.* The allusion is to 'the honours of war' when an army with flags flying and drums beating leaves the scene of successful action.

154

false colours. *pretence to be what one is not*, with reference to a hypocrite or impostor. The words, often used in the expression 'sail under false colours', is nautical, and refers to a ship that approaches its intended prey showing at the mast the false colours of a pretended friendly nation.

155

give (or lend) colour to. *give grounds for believing to be true; provide confirmation of; cause to be plausible.* 'colour' here has a meaning, now obsolete except in this metaphor, of 'show of reason'.

156

like to see the colour of his money. *like to have the money paid:* i.e. to receive, not merely promises, but cash, a cheque, bank notes.

157

nail one's colours to the mast. *adopt an unyielding attitude; refuse to give way, recede, abandon one's principles etc., whatever happens.* The allusion is to nailing a flag to the mast of a ship so that it cannot be lowered in sign of surrender, or have a rope to which it is fixed shot away.

158

off colour. (S) *not well.* A common symptom in a person who is not well is that he is pale, lacking, and so 'off', his usual colour.

159

paint in bright colours. *give a lively and cheerful description of a situation etc.*, or, if there is a reference to the future, *a hopeful interpretation.*

160

put a false colour on. *misinterpret, put a wrong construction on.* For **false colours** (plural) see 154.

161

strike one's colours. *surrender, give in, admit one is beaten.* The metaphor is nautical, and refers to a ship's hauling down its flag. Contrast **come off with flying colours** (153).

162

true colours. *what a person or thing is revealed to be, as* *contrasted with what he or it seemed to be.* Compare **false colours** (154).

163

come a cropper. Literally *have a heavy fall;* figuratively (in which sense it is mostly used) *come to disaster.* It means much the same as **come to grief** (see 168), but it is more colloquial, and it is generally used with a distinctive implication that the disaster is a result of a mistake or of misconduct.

The word 'cropper' is to be found only in this phrase. *S.O.E.D.* suggests that it may be connected with **neck and crop** (618).

164

come down like a ton of bricks. *blame severely in violent terms.*

165

come down on the right side of the fence. This expression, like **sit on the fence** (see 813), came from U.S.A. *make a decision that, of two alternatives, is the right one.* The phrase is generally used with reference to political affairs.

166

come (or get) down to brass tacks. *stop discussing general principles, plans, etc., and turn attention to practical details.* The origin of the metaphor is unknown. I have heard two conjectures. One is that it comes from the building trade, perhaps especially carpentering, and means to turn from big, structural problems, and concern oneself with an immediate practical job of using hammer and nails. The other conjecture is that it comes from accountancy, where a statement of account is considered too general and summary, and needs to be analysed down to small items like the cost of a packet of brass tacks.

Today 'tacks' are called 'tin tacks' (though they are made of iron or steel, not tin), and brass tacks are almost obsolete.

167

come down to earth. *return to thoughts or the discussion of mundane, practical facts and considerations, from lofty, idealistic, visionary reflections.* Compare, for describing the state of a person who has not 'come down to earth', the expression 'in the clouds'.

168

come to grief. *fail, meet with disaster.* The primary meaning of 'grief' is 'deep sorrow', 'keen regret': i.e. an emotion. In 'come to grief' the word means, not an emotion, but the circumstances of failure or disaster that would cause sorrow, regret, etc. The idiom is a common, and, in comparison with many idioms, a simple one, but is given here because it is typical of the continual change that language is undergoing. Dean Alford, writing in the middle of the nineteenth century, mentioned 'come to grief' as a phrase that had only lately ceased to be slang. (See Preface, p. x.)

169

come to. (1) *recover from a fainting fit.* (2) with **oneself,** *return to one's normal, sensible attitude.*

170

when the cows come home. *never.* It is not a fact that cows, when the time comes for them to be milked, fail of their own accord to return from their grazing ground; but they meander extremely slowly to the milking shed, and, even when driven, they will not let themselves be hurried.

171

a contradiction in terms. *a phrase containing words that contradict, that are inconsistent with, one another.* 'A virtuous tyrant [where "tyrant" means an autocratic despot] is a contradiction in terms' (B. Jowett).

172

count one's chickens before they are hatched. *with over-confidence make plans depending on events that may not happen.* The allusion is to a fable by Aesop of a market-woman who said she would sell her eggs, buy a goose, grow rich, then buy a cow, and so on; but in her excitement she kicked over her basket, and all her eggs were broken.

173

crocodile (1) *a* with hypocritical tears of show of grief. The origin of the phrase was the fabulous belief that the animal wept in order to allure or while eating its victims. (2) *n* a line of school girls walking in pairs.

174

cross as two sticks. *annoyed, irritated, petulant.* The origin of the simile is obscure. It has been suggested that the allusion is to two people in a rage who are fighting with sticks. Another explanation is that the expression is a play on words, and refers to two sticks 'crossed' over one another.

175

cross swords (or **measure swords**). *contest a question; enter into* *a dispute or argument.* The phrases are generally used with reference to opposing a rather redoubtable opponent. The metaphors come from duelling. 'measure' here means, in an eighteenth-century sense, 'try one's strength against'.

176

cross (or **pass**) **the Rubicon.** *take a decisive and irrevocable step.* The allusion is to Julius Caesar's act when with his army in 49 B.C. he unconstitutionally crossed the River Rubicon, which separated his province of Cisalpine Gaul from Italy, and so brought on the Civil War.

177

as the crow flies. *in a direct, a straight, the shortest, line between two places.* Compare **bee-line** (49).

178

cry stinking fish. *speak about one's own affairs, circumstances, etc., in a way that reflects unfavourably on oneself.* The implication seems to be that to do this is as stupid as if a man crying (= calling attention to, in order to sell) fish were to announce that it was rotten.

179

cudgel one's brains. *think hard* (to find something to say, to devise a plan, to understand something, etc.). To 'cudgel' is to 'beat (with)', but is archaic except in this expression; as is the noun (for a short, thick stick used as a weapon) except in the figurative phrase 'take up the cudgels for' = 'defend vigorously'. For the use of the word 'cudgel' with reference to 'thinking hard', compare that of 'rack' (literally = 'shake violently') with the same meaning, in 'rack one's brains'.

180

my cup of tea. *the sort of thing that pleases or appeals to me.* The metaphor is nearly always used negatively, for what is not agreeable to one, though sometimes one hears a statement such as 'That's just my cup of tea'. The expression came into use between the First and Second World Wars. In the Victorian age the consumption of tea by all classes had not yet, especially among men, become common. A more likely metaphor then, derived from food or drink for something not to one's taste, would have been, say, 'not my pot of beer', or among the well-to-do classes 'not my glass of wine'. Later the increasing employment of women in offices led to the introduction there of afternoon tea, in which gradually the male members of a staff would join. Later still, what with 'morning tea' in the bedroom, the tendency to substitute tea for coffee at breakfast, and 'elevenses', tea would come to be regarded as a universal social drink. Individual tastes, however, often varied: for China or India tea; weak or strong; with or without milk; with or without sugar; with lemon. This variation would naturally lend itself to the expression 'That is not my cup of tea', and then by extension in general reference to other things that did not suit one's taste: e.g. an entertainment at a theatre, a book, etc., with the meaning 'Whatever others may like, that is not the sort of thing to appeal to me'.

181

cupboard love. *pretence of affection in order to gain material benefit.* 'cupboard', with its store of food, stands for what the pretender aims at getting from the person for whom he simulates affection.

182

in one's cups. *drunk.* (This is a euphemism.) 'cup' today is mostly thought of as a vessel, generally of china, that has a handle, but without a stem (though there is a prize cup, a trophy, that can have one or both or neither), but it used to have a more general meaning that would cover a wine glass.

We'll tak a cup o' kindness yet,
For auld lang syne.

183

curry favour. *ingratiate oneself by flattery.* A strange history is connected with this phrase. There are two verbs to 'curry'. One, from a Tamil word, *kari*, means to flavour meat with spices and ginger. Another verb, derived from an Old French word, *correier*, means to rub down a horse with a curry-comb. In a fourteenth-century satire there is a horse symbolising cunning, called Favel. To 'curry' this creature meant to try to ingratiate oneself with Favel, which became corrupted to 'favour'.

184

a curtain-lecture. *drawn-out complaint by a wife to a husband.* The expression in its literal interpretation meant a reproof in the conjugal bed. The curtain referred to the hangings that used to be round beds.

In the middle of last century the popularity of *Punch* was enhanced by Douglas Jerrold's 'Mrs. Caudle's Curtain-Lectures', which afterwards appeared as a book.

185

cut a dash. *make oneself prominent with one's clothes and other outward belongings* (e.g. *a fine motor-car*). *C.O.D.*, for one meaning of 'cut', gives 'make', and for 'dash' it gives 'showy appearance' (compare the adjective 'dashing').

186

cut a figure. *make a conspicuous appearance.* (That is to say, 'cut' here means 'make' or 'show'.) The expression unqualified implies that one makes an impression that is effective or brilliant; but a person can cut also a 'poor figure', especially by showing up badly in his conduct.

187

cut and dried. The phrase originally referred to herbs, in herbal shops, as contrasted with growing plants, and then came to be applied to (1) opinions, schemes, etc., that are fixed: often derogatorily, narrow and inelastic; (2) detailed and straightforward plans.

188

cut and run. *make haste to get away as soon and quickly as possible* (especially from an unpleasant situation). The metaphor is nautical, for cutting a cable, to make sail instantly without waiting to weigh anchor.

189

cut both ways. *have an advantage that compensates for any disadvantage* (or vice versa). A double-edge sword cuts in two opposite directions.

Compare **It is as broad as it is long** (102).

190

cut it fine. *allow only the minimum of time, material, money, etc., for achieving one's object.* Thus one 'cuts it fine' if one allows so little time to get to the station that one arrives there only a few seconds before the train leaves. The sense of 'cut' nearest to the meaning it has in this expression is 'reduce': e.g. 'cut wages'.

191

cut off one's nose to spite one's face. *from pique, spite, or revenge, do something that will injure oneself.* That is to say, in order to gratify one's resentment, one does something that makes a situation worse. The image is that of a person so dissatisfied, disgusted, annoyed, by his general ugliness that he cuts off one feature, only to make his ugliness worse than it was before.

192

cut off with a shilling. *in a will leave a person nothing.* Brewer says that at one time a testator would include in his will the name of a person he had disinherited, indicating ironically, by leaving him a shilling, that he had not failed to consider his claims.

193

cut one's coat according to one's cloth. *restrict one's expenditure on a particular thing to one's available means, or one's expenditure in general to one's income;* sometimes in a more general sense, *adapt oneself to circumstances.*

The expression is recorded as used as far back as in 1580 by John Lyly.

194

cut one's losses. *resign oneself to;* in another idiom, *write off a loss, on an unprofitable undertaking.* 'cut' here seems to mean 'cut out and remove' the loss from one's accounts as one that cannot be retrieved, and about which nothing more can be done. Compare **throw good money after bad** (458).

195

cut out. (1) As a participial adjective meaning *suitable.* '**I** never thought her cut out for office work.' (2) As a verb = *supplant*. 'Nevertheless she easily cut out all the other clerks in her reputation for industry and punctuality.' (3) As a verb (naval), meaning *capture* a ship by cutting its cable, etc. (4) As a participial adjective with reference to a task there may be difficulty in executing. 'I shall have my work cut out to finish that job by the end of this week.' 'You will have your work cut out to satisfy that manager.' Perhaps this is a tailoring metaphor, with reference to the difficulty a tailor may have in cutting an amount of cloth so as to make it serve for a garment or garments.

196

Cut the cackle and come to the horses (or **'osses**). *Shorten the general talk about the situation, and deal with the heart of the matter*. 'cackle' (or 'cackling') is the noise made by a hen, especially after laying an egg. For 'cut' here compare 'cut down', 'cut short'. The origin of the second part of the expression, 'and come to the horses', is unknown. Compare **come down to brass tacks** (166).

A friend tells me that an explanation he has heard is that 'cackle' is a corruption of 'cattle', and that the expression comes from impatient horse-buyers at market, and means 'Don't trouble about such comparative trivialities as cattle. Sell the horses first.'

197

cut the Gordian knot. *solve a complicated difficulty by quick and drastic action.* The allusion is to a story about Gordius, a peasant of ancient Phrygia, and Alexander the Great. An oracle declared that disturbances in the country would be ended by a wagon. When Gordius, arriving in a wagon, was chosen as king, he dedicated it to Zeus. Its pole was fastened to the yoke by a sort of bark. An oracle declared moreover that whoever untied the knot would reign over Asia. When in a later age Alexander in his conquests came to Phrygia, and heard about the oracle, he cut the knot with his sword.

198

cut to the quick. *deeply hurt in one's feelings.* The 'quick' (an old Saxon word) is the tender sensitive flesh below the skin and especially the nails.

199

cut up rough. *show annoyance and resentment.* (OO)

200

damn with faint praise. *express one's praise of a person in such luke-warm terms that it is nearer condemnation than approval.* The phrase comes from Pope's 'Epistle to Dr. Arbuthnot', in his attack on Addison, as one who would

> Damn with faint praise, assent with civil leer,
> And, without sneering, teach the rest to sneer.

201

a damp squib. *intended joke or entertainment that fails in its effect.* A 'squib' is a firework; if it is damp it will not send out sparks.

202

a Darby and Joan. *an example of an old and devoted married couple.* Brewer refers to two couples who were stated to be the originals of the expression. He says the characters belong to a ballad by Henry Woodfall. I have been unable to trace this composer in the catalogue of the British Museum, or in the *Dictionary of National Biography.* There are several songs entitled 'Darby and Joan' in the British Museum, of which the earliest was composed by one I. Barker and is thought to have been published in 1800.

203

a dark horse. *a person whose capabilities are unknown, and whose future career cannot be surmised.* The term is from horse-racing, for a horse about whose racing capabilities little or nothing is known. 'dark' refers, not to a horse with dark hair, but to people being 'in the dark' about it.

204

The darkest place is under the candlestick. *The person primarily concerned in an affair often has the least information about it.* The principal of a firm or some other organisation, who one might have expected to be more intimately conversant with all the most intimate secrets than anybody else, is often surprisingly ignorant of what is common knowledge among the general mass of minor subordinates.

205

any day. Taken in its ordinary literal sense and at the face value of the words, this phrase refers only to time. 'He may arrive any day.' But colloquially it is often used to mean *in any circumstances*, and generally with an implication of preference of one thing or person to one or more alternatives. 'I prefer any day to know the worst to being buoyed up by false hopes.'

206

call it a day. (S) *consider the day's work as finished.*

207

day in and day out or day in, day out. *every day, day after day:* i.e. as, in succession, each day comes *in*, and, ending, goes *out*, to be in its turn followed by another. Variants of 'day', but less common, are 'week', 'month', 'year'.

208

for a rainy day. *for circumstances in the future when money that has been saved or reserved may be needed.*

209

His (or **Its**) **days are numbered.** *His* (or *Its*) *death* or *end is near and inevitable.* In this expression the verb 'number', in the passive, has a special meaning of 'restricted in number'.

210

palmy days. *flourishing period.* 'palmy' = 'worthy to wear the palm'. In ancient times a branch of the palm tree was carried, or a leaf of it worn, as a symbol of victory or triumph. An expression 'to bear the palm', now obsolescent, means 'to be the best', 'be the winner'.

211

pass the time of day. This phrase is now, except colloquially, archaic, but is often to be found in books of the last century and earlier. The words 'the time of day' stand for 'a little time' (or a part) of the day, to be passed, spent, with a person in exchanging salutations or in a friendly chat.

212

seen better days. *experienced more prosperous times.* See *Timon of Athens*, IV, ii.

213

the day (or **a day**) **after the fair.** *too late.* The phrase refers to something that might have been done, but now cannot be, as the opportunity has been lost and will not recur. It goes back in this sense to 1548.

214

dead as a door-nail. *quite dead. O.E.D.* defines 'door-nail' as a large-headed nail with which doors were formerly studded. Why it was taken as typical of lifelessness is obscure. Stevenson cites its use as far back as the fourteenth-century romance *William of Palerne.* In 2 *Henry VI* (IV, x) Jack Cade says 'if I do not leave you all as dead as a door-nail, I pray God I may never eat grass more'.

215

dead as mutton. *quite dead.* In this simile 'dead' is used only figuratively, because among living organisms there can be no degree of being dead. That is to say, the expression refers only to things that are past, obsolete, out of fashion, not effective, etc. 'as mutton' is used only as an emphasiser, 'mutton' being the flesh of a dead, as contrasted with a living, sheep; but why 'mutton' rather than 'beef' is obscure.

216

a dead letter. (1) *law or rule not enforced.* (2) The Dead Letter Office is the department of the Post Office from which letters that cannot be delivered are, if possible, returned to their writers.

217

dead men's shoes. *expectations of money to be inherited.*

218

dead sea fruit. *something of illusory beauty or attraction that turns out to be a hollow and bitter disappointment.*

From time immemorial there were tales of a strange fruit that was said to grow on the shores of the Dead Sea. Josephus, in the first century A.D., wrote of it, as having a fair appearance externally, but, when grasped, breaking into ashes or powder.

219

die game. *maintain a resolute attitude to the end of a struggle.* The expression might be used for literally fighting to the end, but it is generally applied in a figurative sense, especially with reference to a political or moral cause. The phrase is from cock-fighting. Cocks bred for fighting were called 'game-cocks', and 'game' came to be used as an adjective, meaning 'like a game-cock', i.e. 'spirited'.

220

a die-hard. The term, generally applied to a politician, means a person who, however much general opinion round him has changed, refuses to change or compromise: i.e. he will not let his opinions, figuratively, 'die'.

221

give up the ghost. *die.* 'ghost' once meant the principle of life. (See *Job.* 14, 10.) This sense is retained in the term Holy Ghost. The phrase is also used facetiously for things breaking up and being no longer of use.

222

go west. *die.* The original allusion was to the sinking of the sun in the west. This was probably reinforced during pioneering days in U.S. when men moving westwards were often not heard of again. The phrase became popularised here in the First World War, based, no doubt by American influence, on the westward transport of dying and dead soldiers.

223

hang on like grim death. *stick resolutely to the task in hand, whatever the difficulties.* Death is taken as a symbol of a force that, having seized its victim, never relaxes its hold.

224

in at the death. *in time to see or take part in the climax of an affair.* The metaphor is from fox-hunting, where a huntsman arrives in time to see the fox killed. See **run to earth** (751).

225

kick the bucket. (S) *O.E.D.* gives a quotation from a newspaper that says 'bucket' was used in Norfolk for the beam on which a pig was hung by its heels after it had been killed, and that this was the origin of the use of 'kick the bucket' to mean 'die'. Neither the title nor date of the newspaper is mentioned, but I am indebted to Mr. D. M. Davin of the Clarendon Press for the information that the date was probably about 1880.

226

pass away. *die.* 'pass away' is either a genteelism or rather smug euphemism, or is deliberately used by those who think the phrase is more consonant than 'die' with the belief in a future life. There are some who use 'pass over'.

227

passing. *death.* Unless 'passing' is used with a sort of religious implication, it is, today, like 'pass away' (see last article), a genteelism or smug euphemism. Henley in a poem had the line 'So be my passing'. But what may have been good idiom in one age may become not so in another.

228

to the death. (literally) *until one of the combatants is killed;* (figuratively, with reference to resisting some policy etc.) *vehemently to the end without surrender.*

229

turn up one's toes. *die.* When a corpse, in the death position, is on its back, the toes are turned upwards.

230

the deepest dye. *extreme badness.* 'deepest' means 'most intense': compare e.g. 'The colour of this rose is deep red'. The phrase does not specify what colour a scoundrel or crime of the 'deepest dye' is supposed to be, but probably most of us would imagine it to be black.

231

out of one's depth. *beyond one's knowledge*, or *beyond one's understanding*. The allusion is to water that is too deep for one to be able to keep one's footing or not to be submerged. Compare **head over ears** (492).

232

between the devil and the deep sea. *between two equally serious evils or dangers.* Perhaps originally the implied contrast was that of being burnt by the devil in hell fire and being drowned.

Compare **between Scylla and Charybdis** (774).

233

play the (or **the very**) **devil** (or **deuce**) **with.** *injure.* 'play' means 'play the part of', as in e.g. 'play the fool', 'play the man'. 'deuce', used here as a synonym of 'devil', is used also, with sense of 'bad luck' etc., in imprecations: 'the deuce', 'what the deuce' (alternatives of 'the devil', 'what the devil'). It is probably connected etymologically with the other meaning of 'deuce', which goes back much further, for the 'two' at dice and cards.

234

the devil to pay. *a heavy price or reckoning.* The allusion is to the Faust legend of the heavy price exacted by the devil for favours had from him. The devil takes Faust to hell.

235

to give the devil his due. *do justice to a person one dislikes by admitting a point in his favour.*

236

the Dickens is an exclamatory term to express indignation, annoyance, impatience, etc., or merely to emphasise. 'I don't know who the Dickens he is'; 'He made the Dickens of a row about it'. *O.E.D.* suggests that the phrase is a corruption of a diminutive of 'devil': 'devilkin' becoming 'de'ilkin', and then 'dickin', and finally 'Dickens'.

Shakespeare has 'I can't tell what the dickens his name is' (*The Merry Wives of Windsor*, III, ii).

237

do in Rome as the Romans do. *adapt yourself to the customs and manners of those you live among or are closely associated with.* The *Oxford Dictionary of English Proverbs* cites St. Ambrose (340–97) for an injunction on which the proverb is based = *Si fueris Romae, Romano vivito more; si fueris alibi, vivito sicut ibi* ('If you are in Rome, live in the Roman way; if you are elsewhere, live as they do there'). Records of the proverb in English go back to the sixteenth century.

238

a dog in the manger. *a churlish person who, though he does not want, or is unable to have, something, grudges or prevents its being had by others.* The phrase comes from Aesop's fable of the dog that, though it had no use for the hay in the manger, growled at the horses and would not let them eat it.

239

a dog's life. *a wretched unpleasant existence*, especially one that is harassed by over-work or ill-treatment or poverty. Sir Alan Herbert in a delightful poem in *Punch* has pointed out the unsuitability of the expression to the life led by dogs today in this country.

He leads a dog's life, people say–
But why?
Who has a better life than thou,
Bow-wow?
For every hound
Free food is found,
Without the harsh behest we meet,
That we must work before we eat.
All day you do exactly as you feel;
You sleep before, and after, every meal.
Things would be said,
If I had as much bed.*

In distinction to the idea conveyed in 'a dog's life' we have the expression 'a gay dog' for a light-hearted sporting man leading a life of pleasure and amusement.

* From 'Horse-talk with a Dog', reproduced by leave of Sir Alan Herbert and the Proprietors of *Punch*.

240

Dog does not eat dog. *A person ought not to attack, try to injure, try to make profit out of, a person of his own set:* e.g. one in the same occupation, with the same interests, working in the same cause. Thus a doctor does not charge a fee to another doctor.

241

dog-tired. *extremely tired.* When a dog comes in tired it flops down as if dead.

242

go to the dogs. *take to bad courses with bad companions; lead an irregular life that will end in ruin.* The selection of dogs as typical of creatures living disorderly lives probably reflects biblical influence. In the Bible the dog appears, not as the friend of man, but as an unclean and degraded creature. 'Give not that which is holy unto the dogs, neither cast ye your pearls before swine.' 'Beware of dogs, beware of evil workers.' 'For without are dogs, and sorcerers, and whoremongers, and murderers, and idolaters.' 'Is thy servant a dog that he should do this great thing?' says Hazaël to Elisha, who has prophesied the abominations he will do to the children of Israel. Sir John Bland-Sutton, in *Selected Lectures and Essays* (1920), telling the story of Tobit, from the *Apocrypha*, says the dog that accompanied Tobias on his journey to Ecbatana (which he thinks may be the origin of Dog Toby in *Punch and Judy*) is the only one to receive favourable mention in the Bible.

S.O.E.D. gives 'dog' as in Middle English being used with a meaning of 'worthless fellow'.

Among the ancient Greeks and Romans the dog was in general regarded as the devoted and helpful friend of man. A celebrated and moving reference to one comes in Homer's

Odyssey, where Argos, Ulysses' old dog, recognises his master on his return, wags his tail, and dies.

In contrast to this general attitude to dogs in Greek and Roman antiquity, as the devoted and helpful friend of man, the sect of Greek philosophers founded by Antisthenes were given the name of Cynics (from the Greek word *kuon* = 'a dog') because they were regarded as shameless for their behaviour in following the precept of Diogenes that everything that was natural was right, and therefore one should not hesitate to do it in public.

243

Let sleeping dogs lie. *Do not disturb a state of affairs with potentialities of harm at present dormant, lest action may precipitate trouble.* The phrase is adumbrated in Chaucer.

244

a cat and dog life. *a relation, between two people, of constant bickering and quarrelling,* especially between husband and wife. Dogs and cats are traditional enemies.

245

a cat's-paw. *a person used as a tool by another.* The allusion is to a fable about a monkey that wished to get some chestnuts from the fire without burning itself, and used the paw of a cat.

246

get (or put) a person's back up. *make him annoyed.* The metaphor is of the way a cat arches its back when annoyed.

247

let the cat out of the bag. *divulge a secret, especially inadvertently.* Brewer says that formerly country folk going to market would sometimes put a cat in a bag (or 'poke') that they pretended held a sucking-pig, hoping to impose this on a greenhorn who would buy it without examination; but, if the intending buyer opened the bag, the trick was disclosed. See **buy a pig in a poke** (113).

248

not room to swing a cat. (One has, there is) *extremely little space.* Many conjectures have been made about the origin of the expression. One is that it refers to a former barbarous custom of suspending a cat in a bag or leathern bottle at which arrows were shot. (Cf. *Much Ado about Nothing*, I, i: 'If I do, hang me in a bottle like a cat and shoot at me'.) Another conjecture is that 'cat' is an abbreviation of 'cat-o'-nine tails', a whip with nine lashes used for punishing offenders. An objection to this explanation is that 'cat' was not used with this meaning until long after the expression was common. A third explanation is that the allusion was to the practice of sailors 'swinging' (= 'hanging') their hammocks or cots within a confined space in a ship, and that 'cat' was a corruption of 'cot'. A fourth explanation offered during a recent correspondence in *The Times* was that the allusion was to a small cargo boat swinging at her moorings.

249

rain cats and dogs. *rain heavily.* Cats and dogs, notorious for their hostility to one another—scratching and biting, hissing and growling—create an uproar that becomes a metaphor for a heavy downpour of rain. The first recorded use of the expression goes back two hundred years.

250

rub a person up the wrong way. *annoy, offend, a person.* The allusion may be to the dislike a cat shows when its fur is stroked the wrong way. *S.O.E.D.* cites the use of the phrase with the meaning 'annoy', 'irritate', as far back as 1523.

251

see how the cat jumps. *wait until one finds what happens in connection with some matter before making a decision what course to take.* The expression is often used with reference to a politician refusing to commit himself to the formulation of his policy until public opinion has declared itself. It is not much more than a hundred years old.

252

sick as a cat; sick as a dog. *extremely sick.* In these similes 'sick' means 'vomiting'. The dog and cat, being our chief animal friends, are the two animals whose behaviour is most familiar to us, but there are no grounds for imagining that they are more violently sick than other animals.

(There is a verb 'cat', used colloquially to mean 'vomit'.)

253

in the doldrums. *depressed.* The Doldrums are a region of the ocean near the equator, where there is so little wind that sailing ships were often becalmed.

254

donkey-work. *subordinate work.* The expression is often used with reference to work, and often onerous work, a person has to do that is much below his abilities. The phrase may be connected with a 'donkey-man' or 'donkey-boy', who has the rather humble duties of being in charge of a donkey; or with a 'donkey-engine', which is a small engine on a ship used for subsidiary operations such as feeding the boilers of the propelling engines.

255

donkey's years. *a long time.* Brewer says that the allusion is to an old tradition that one never saw a dead donkey. Another suggestion is that the phrase is a play on words: 'donkey's years' for 'donkey's ears', which are long.

256

dot one's i's and cross one's t's. *be most punctiliously precise in the minutest details.* The allusion is no doubt to the instructions given by an imaginary teacher to pupils learning to write. Compare **mind one's P's and Q's** (606).

257

down and out. *utterly destitute.* The metaphor is from boxing when a defeated boxer has been knocked down and is unable to rise to resume the fight before he is counted out.

258

down at heel. *shabbily dressed and in a state of poverty.* Heels of shoes that are worn down are taken as emblematic of a poverty-stricken appearance.

Other metaphors in which poverty is indicated by the state of a person's clothes are **on one's uppers** (976), there too referring to foot-wear, and **out at elbow** (277).

259

down in the mouth. *depressed.* There is a tendency, when one is in low spirits, for the corners of the mouth to drop, as conversely there is, when one is cheerful, for them to go up. Compare the expression **pull a long face** (309), and **keep a stiff upper lip** (529).

260

draw a bow at a venture. Literally, *not aim at an object, but hope to hit something;* and so figuratively *say something on the chance that what one half suspects may be found to be true*. The phrase comes from the Bible in a passage about the death of Ahab: 'A certain man drew a bow at a venture and smote the King of Israel' (I *Kings*, 22, 34).

261

draw the long bow. *exaggerate.* The long-bow of the medieval soldier, discharging long, feathered arrows, was drawn by hand (as contrasted with the cross-bow, which had a mechanism for releasing the string), and the force of the missile depended on that of the arm drawing the bow. So metaphorically the force of a statement made by a person who exaggerates depends on his inventive imagination.

262

Draw it mild. *Do not exaggerate.* In a public bar a common distinction between varieties of beer that the barmaid or barman draws is that of 'mild' and 'bitter'. 'bitter' is the stronger. In an idiom based on this variety a person telling an incredible story is admonished to 'draw it mild'.

263

dressed up to the nines. *dressed to perfection.* 'up to the nines' is not used in any other context. *S.O.E.D.* says the phrase goes back to the end of the eighteenth century. (OO)

264

drink like a fish. *be a drunkard.* The simile dates back as far as the middle of the seventeenth century, where it is found in Shirley's *The Triumph of Beauty*. Brewer points out that many fish swim with their mouths open, but it is considered today that they drink little water, if any.

265

drop a brick. *in conversation or speech or letter, suddenly, unexpectedly, startlingly, to come out with a remark that excites strong disagreement and disapproval and dismay.* The reference is often to a remark that is an indiscretion rather than one intended to cause trouble.

266

a drug on the market. *something not in demand, as the supply of it is larger than is needed.* The phrase can refer to other things than material commodities. (OO)

267

not so dusty. (S) *not too bad; fairly good.*

268

Dutch courage. *courage induced by drink.* Mr. Eric Partridge says the original reference in the phrase was to the heavy drinking by Dutch soldiers in former times. Waller (1665) has

The Dutch their wine and all their brandy lose,
Disarmed of that from which their courage grows.

269

on earth. This phrase, used with the pronouns 'who' and 'what' and a number of adverbs, 'when', 'where', 'why', 'how', is an emphasiser that corresponds to the suffix '-ever'. 'How on earth [However] did you manage to do that?' 'I had no idea what on earth [whatever] he was driving at.'

270

Dog does not eat dog: see 240.

271

eat humble pie. *submit meekly and apologetically* to blame or humiliation. 'humble pie' is thought to be either a perversion of, or a play on, 'umbles', the edible inward, and less prized, parts of an animal, usually a deer, which Brewer says were in a baron's household made into a pie for the huntsman and other retainers who sat at the lower end of the table in the hall where meals were served.

272

eat one's cake and have it. This metaphor is always used either negatively: e.g. 'one cannot eat one's cake and (still) have it', or ironically: e.g. 'He wants to eat his cake and have it', signifying the impossibility of reaping the advantages of two opposed courses of conduct. Thus one cannot indulge in the pleasure of spending money freely and at the same time enjoy the satisfaction of saving money. The expression can be compared, as Mr. Eric Partridge says, with 'You cannot have it both ways'.

273

eat one's heart out. *have one's emotional life absorbed by deep and continuous grief.* (For the form of the expression compare 'cry one's eyes out'.) 'out' is a modern addition to the expression. The first recorded use of the metaphor in English (it goes back to Homer) by John Lyly in 1579 has 'Not to eat our heartes'; and 'out' does not appear in Spenser's *Faerie Queene*; Thomas Draxe's collection of proverbs (1616); Burton's *Anatomy of Melancholy*; Bacon's *Essays.*

274

eat one's words. *ignominiously retract what one has said.* The image is that of a person, out of whose mouth the given words have gone, recovering, chewing, and swallowing them.

275

The proof of the pudding is in the eating. *It is only experience of the results that will show the value of some arrangement, plan, theory, etc.;* in the same way that only the eating and tasting of a pudding proves how good the ingredients were and how skilful the cooking of it has been.
The first recorded use of the saying is by Henry Glapthorne in 1635, and the second by Addison in 1714.

276

elbow grease: generally used with 'needs plenty of', 'put plenty of (into)'. *hard manual work.* In the phrase there is a transference of the idea of a lubricant used for machinery to that of perspiration caused by vigorous manual work.
For 'elbow' see also the next article and 609.

277

out at elbow(s). *shabbily dressed and in a state of poverty.* For other metaphors indicating poverty as shown by the state of a person's clothes see **down at heel** (258) and **on one's uppers** (976). For 'elbow' see also the last article and 609.

278

at the eleventh hour. *at the latest possible time. S.O.E.D.* refers the origin of the phrase in this sense to a passage in the Bible (*Matthew*, 20), in the parable of the labourers in the vineyard. 'eleventh hour' are the words used for the time, in a twelve hours' working day, when the last batch of labourers were engaged.

279

at a loose end. *without any particular work to do:* often with the additional idea that one is discontented because of that. Perhaps the metaphor is a nautical one, and refers to a rope that, being at one end untied to something, is not serving any purpose.

Compare **kick one's heels** (535) and **twiddle one's thumbs** (972); but, whereas those two expressions most probably refer to a short period of time, some minutes, hours, or at the most some days, 'being at a loose end' might extend over a comparatively long period.

280

burn the candle at both ends: see 109.

281

end in smoke. *have no result; come to nothing.* The idea is that one's expectations of a bright fire with flame are disappointed.

282

go off the deep end. *get into a state of violent emotion of love, anger, etc.* This is a figurative extension of the image of a person's diving into deep water in a swimming-bath.

283

make ends (or both ends) meet. *live within one's income.* The two ends are expenditure and income, which are regarded as coming together so as not to leave a gap: perhaps like the cloth of a coat stretched to make a good fit.

284

make one's hair stand on end. *cause extreme horror.* Human beings vary in the degree in which they show, as well as in their capacity for feeling, emotion, but all mammals have under their skin small muscles pulling on hairs, which can be held nearly upright, especially under the influence of fear or when they feel cold. The technical name for this physiological reaction is 'pilomotor', and there is a long description of it in Charles Darwin's *Expression of Emotion in Man and Animals.* To Professor E. G. T. Liddell I am indebted for a letter on this matter, with reference to the phrase 'make one's hair stand on end', in which he says 'If you ever have the opportunity of watching a short-coated, highly-strung dog like a light coloured dachshund approaching a potential enemy, you will have a good view of erection of hairs'.

285

on one's beam-ends: see 39.

286

the end of one's tether. *limit of one's powers of endurance.* The allusion is to an animal: e.g. a goat, tied to a rope or chain beyond the length of which it cannot graze.

287

the fag-end. *the extreme finish, or the last numerically:* e.g. of a task, the cricket season, a store of articles that are at last coming to an end. 'fag' was used as far back as the seventeenth century for the last part of a piece of cloth. Towards the end of the nineteenth century it came to be abbreviated in slang to 'fag', for a cigarette.

288

the thin end of the wedge. *an action that, though it may* *seem small and unimportant, may lead to serious developments.* The metaphor is that of a piece of wood or metal used to split wood or rock, or to widen an opening, or exert force in various ways.

289

the wrong end of the stick. (S) *an assumption, interpretation, theory, approach in an argument, view of a situation, etc., that is the exact reverse of the right one.* Perhaps the allusion was to the simple act of holding a walking-stick by its lower end, which in right use would be on the ground, instead of by its upper end or handle: i.e. holding it upside-down. I am told, however, by the Rev. H. Lupton, that he can remember that in his earlier days in Lincolnshire and Yorkshire villages a common expression was 'the dirty end of the stick', referring to a stick used to stir human ordure in a pit before the time of even earth-closets.

290

to the bitter end: see 60.

291

enough rope. (1) *sufficient freedom and independence to allow scope for initiative.* (2) The proverb 'Give a man rope enough and he will hang himself' means 'Let him continue his misdoings until he reaps the consequences'. The allusion may be to a grazing animal tethered by a rope (see 286).

292

all my eye (or **all in my eye**): see 9.

293

cast sheep's eyes. *cast amorous glances of a half-furtive sort.* A sheep generally looks sideways. The phrase has also the implication of awkwardness, shyness, embarrassment, that 'sheepishness' and 'sheepish' bear.

294

see eye to eye (with). *be of the same mind (as).* The idea underlying this expression, as it is used, is that one person with his 'eye' (= 'eyes': a common substitute of the singular for the plural) sees things differently from another person, and, figuratively, holds a different opinion. Compare the phrase 'see in the same light'. In this sense 'to' can be regarded as an elision for 'close to' (compare 'shoulder to shoulder', 'heart to heart', 'hand to hand', etc.). When A's and B's eyes are close to one another, they see an object from almost the same angle, and may therefore get the same impression. Henry Bradley, however, in *The Making of English*, has pointed out that, though the phrase has assumed the character of an English idiom, in the sense here given, this application of it has no warrant in the original context, where it is a translation in the Bible (*Isaiah*, 52, 8) of the Hebrew, and is there used of people, not literally seeing the same thing, nor, figuratively, thinking the same thing, but looking at one another eye to eye, face to face.

This sort of thing, says Bradley, has happened to many biblical phrases, for the most part renderings of Hebrew and Greek, that are often used with little or no consciousness of their origin.

295

the apple of one's eye: see 23.

296

The scales fell from his eyes. *He now saw the situation, facts, etc., clearly.* This meaning of 'scales' as, metaphorically, something that prevents one from recognising realities, has come from a passage in the Bible (*Acts*, 9, 18), where St. Paul is visited by Ananias. 'And immediately there fell from his eyes as it had been scales: and he received sight forthwith and arose and was baptised.' 'as it were scales': like the membraneous or horny modifications of the skin forming a covering of the body in many fishes and reptiles; and 'scales' were taken later as a type of that which causes blindness physical or moral.

297

throw dust in a person's eyes. *do or say something that will mislead by misrepresentation, or divert attention from a point:* i.e. figuratively impair a person's vision so that he cannot see things clearly. The metaphor is recorded as being used early in the seventeenth century.

298

up to the eyes. *deeply engaged* (in work). The metaphor is that of a person who is deeply plunged in a mass of work. Perhaps there is an image of being in water almost out of one's depth.

299

with half an eye. When the object is material the meaning is *with merely a hurried casual glance; without close inspection:* keeping one's eyes, as it were, only half open. But the phrase is more often used figuratively, meaning *with merely superficial consideration,* especially of a matter that is obvious.

300

with one's eyes open. *fully aware of all the circumstances; without any illusions.*

301

cut off one's nose to spite one's face: see 191.

Many of the following idioms are based on the idea that a person's thoughts, feelings, words, and actions are reflected in the expression on his face.

302

fly in the face of. *openly disobey.* The literal meaning of 'in the face of' is that a thing is done in a person's sight: with the eyes in the person's face looking at, directly opposite to, in front of, confronting, one; and so figuratively in direct opposition to, in defiance of. 'fly' gives a sense of flagrantly rushing on. Compare the use of the verb in 'fly at' = 'attack'.

A special extension of the phrase is 'fly in the face of providence'. This means do something that is almost bound to bring trouble on oneself. 'providence' is the spirit of foreseeing beneficence in God or nature that is assumed to preside over man's fate. The Stoics believed in a spirit of beneficence that would cease to protect a person if he made excessive demands on the amount of good fortune he could reasonably expect.

An idiom with a similar meaning is 'tempt providence'. 'tempt' here is used in the biblical and now archaic sense of 'provoke', 'defy'. Compare Christ's words to Satan (*Luke*, 4, 12): 'Thou shalt not tempt the Lord thy God'.

303

have the face. *have the effrontery, insolence,* (S) *cheek.* The meaning of the phrase is a figurative extension of the idea that a person makes no change in the expression of his face when doing or saying something that one might expect would cause him to be shamefaced. Compare the phrase 'brazen-faced'.

304

in the face (of). For **fly in the face of** = 'disobey' see 302. Apart from that expression, **in the face (of)** means (1) *in spite (of)*; (2) *in view (of)*; *in consideration (of)*.

305

keep a straight face. *C.O.D.* defines 'straight face' as one 'intentionally inexpressive'. The idea in the phrase seems to be that the lines of the face are kept rigid. It is generally used to mean that one deliberately avoids showing by altering the expression on the face that one thinks something is false or absurd.

306

laugh on the wrong side of his mouth (or **other side of his face**). *be unpleasantly surprised to find that matters are different from what were confidently imagined or expected.* The expressions cannot be analysed so that the literal meaning of the words makes sense, as we do not laugh or smile on one side of our mouth or face, and show displeasure on the other. Recorded uses of these expressions go back to the seventeenth century.

307

lose face. (This is a translation of a Chinese phrase, *tiu lien.*) *be discredited, be humiliated, suffer loss of prestige.* The metaphor is based on the idea that a person, when things have not gone well with him through a set-back, rebuff, failure of plans, diplomatic defeat, etc., no longer goes about with a self-confident bearing, but has a hang-dog expression on his face that his opponents will notice and interpret to his discredit. The phrase is generally used with reference to relations between countries.

308

on the face of it. *as it appears; at first sight; to go by what has been said or written.* The phrase is often used with reference to something the speaker or writer suspects is not what it seems to be.

309

pull (or **draw** or **wear**) **a long face.** *show concern or disapproval by a serious facial expression.* When people are strongly moved by concern or disapproval there is a tendency for the lines of the face to be 'pulled' down, as contrasted with their being broadened and rounded under the influence of pleasant emotions. Compare **keep a straight face** (305).

310

put a bold face on. *show an undaunted spirit about* (some difficulty, trouble, etc.).

311

put a good face on. (in discussing a difficulty, trouble, etc.) *interpret it in a cheerful or hopeful or acquiescent spirit.*

312

save one's face. *manage to escape discredit, to maintain one's reputation.* Compare **lose face** (307).

313

set one's face against. *firmly oppose* (*action, plan, etc.*) Here the lines of the face are set in a sternly unbending expression. The phrase appears in *Leviticus*, 20, 3.

314

show one's face. *appear on the scene.*

315

throw in a person's face. *reproach, blame, a person.* Compare **cast** (or **throw** or **fling**) **in a person's teeth** (125).

316

face about. *say* or *do something that is the reverse of what one was saying or doing before.* The metaphor is a military one from the operation when soldiers make an 'about turn' in the opposite direction to that in which they were standing or marching.

317

face it out. *confront and cope with a difficult situation in a confident spirit.* The phrase can moreover in some contexts have an implication of defiantly refusing to admit one is in a weak position, or has made a mistake or done wrong.

318

face the music. *meet a crisis or criticism boldly without flinching.* The link between the words taken literally and the meaning of the phrase baffles conjecture unless 'music' is used ironically for 'unpleasant noise', 'row' (which has a colloquial meaning of 'disturbance', 'commotion').

319

face up to. *recognise and take action to cope with a difficult situation.* The would-be purists deprecate the use of the three words 'face up to' as a pleonasm meaning no more than the one word 'face'. There are, however, contexts in which 'face up to' can have a distinctive and useful sense. 'face' by itself may denote merely that one is in the presence of, in face of, confronted by, literally a person or thing, figuratively a circumstance, especially a difficulty. 'As he entered the room, he faced the anxious questioning gaze of a hundred eyes.' 'They now faced a fresh problem.' But 'face up to' can imply that a person not only is in the presence of a difficulty but recognises it as a difficulty and takes action to try to overcome it. 'He faced up to these new and unexpected embarrassments with his usual courage and ingenuity.' 'He would never face up to the need of drastic economy if he was to escape bankruptcy.'

320

two-faced; double-faced. *deceitful; pretending to be one thing when one is another; showing duplicity:* e.g. saying one thing to A, and a contrary thing to B.

321

the fag-end: see 287.

322

is (or **sounds** or **reads**) **like a fairy tale.** *is a romantic story of extraordinary good fortune and happiness.*

323

fall between two stools. *fail through taking an intermediate course*, between two courses, whereas success might have come by boldly going for either one or the other. The French have a similar expression: *être assis entre deux chaises*—'to sit between two chairs'. The image is that of a person who, having a choice of two stools for his seat, refuses both, and falls on the ground between them.

324

fall foul of. *get into angry relations with, quarrel with.* The metaphor is a nautical one, for a ship that runs into another or into anything floating or submerged in its way.

325

fall on one's feet. *find oneself in satisfactory circumstances,* especially when danger and difficulty might have been feared or expected. If a person drops from a height on his feet he is in most circumstances less likely to be seriously injured than if he falls otherwise. Alternatively the allusion may be to a cat, which always falls on its feet.

326

The scales fell from his eyes: see 296.

327

a far cry from. *widely different from; only remotely connected with.* 'It is a far cry from having a general sympathy with socialistic principles to becoming a full-fledged member of the Communist Party.' Literally a 'far cry' reaching B from A would mean that there was a great distance between A and B.

328

The fat was in the fire. *This* (*something said or done*) *provoked an explosion of anger;* or *This led to great disturbance and trouble.* The image is that of grease, in which something is being fried, falling out of the pan on to the burning coals, and causing flame and smoke and spluttering. Compare **Then the band played** (36) and **Then the balloon went up** (34).

The early use of the phrase expressed, not an explosion, but failure. There is a record of it as far back as the middle of the sixteenth century.

329

birds of a feather. *people of the same sort.* There is a proverb 'Birds of a feather flock together'. For this use of 'feather' compare *Timon of Athens*, I, i, 101:

> I am not of that feather to shake off
> My friend when he must need me.

330

a feather in his cap: see 116.

331

feather one's nest. *take advantage of one's opportunities, in occupation, situation, relations with people, etc., to benefit oneself, especially monetarily.* The allusion is to birds lining their nests with feathers they collect from the ground. The use of the expression goes back to 1553.

332

Fine feathers make fine birds. *To be well dressed gives one an impressive appearance.* This expression is generally used with an implication that, as in a bird fine plumage is not the only consideration of merit (there may be, for example, the considerations whether it is adequately fat and tender), so, in well-dressed people, a fine appearance may only superficially cover a bad character, stupidity, etc.

The original form of this proverbial idiom had 'Fair feathers make fair fowls'. There is a record of this as far back as 1611. The first record of the current form is a hundred years later.

333

in fine (or **good** or **grand** or **full** or **high**) **feather.** *in excellent health, or spirits, or health and spirits.* The metaphors come from birds, whose condition is shown by the appearance of their feathers. 'full' would mean 'thick'.

'high' perhaps refers to the raised effect of the plumage of a healthy bird contrasted with the limp, flaccid appearance of that of an ailing one.

334

ruffle a person's feathers. *annoy a person.* 'ruffle' means to 'disturb the smoothness of', literally and figuratively: e.g. a person's hair, a person's feelings. The allusion is to birds which, when angry, ruffle up their feathers. Compare **smooth one's rumpled feathers** (336).

335

show the white feather. *be cowardly.* The allusion is to cock fighting. A white feather in a game-cock's plumage denoted bad breeding.

336

smooth one's rumpled feathers. *regain one's equanimity.* Compare **ruffle a person's feathers** (334). 'ruffle' and 'rumple' can have the same meaning, of 'disorder', 'make uneven', but it is one of the peculiarities of language that, whereas with reference to annoying another the word used is 'ruffle' (see 334), with reference to recovering one's composure it is 'rumple'.

337

fed up. (S) *bored to the point of irritation.* Pearsall Smith says the expression is probably derived from the 'feeding' of agricultural machines. There is also an extension of the phrase: 'fed up to the teeth'. If Pearsall Smith's conjecture is right, the addition of 'to the teeth' would have been added later by somebody who thought 'fed up' referred to a person who had eaten too much food.

338

feel in one's bones. *have a strong conviction apart from, and perhaps not supported by, reasons one could formulate.* One 'feels' it rather than 'thinks' it. *C.O.D.* defines the meaning of the phrase as 'have vague or emotional conviction'. It is a strange expression, because it is meant to express the idea that the conviction is deep down in one's inner being. It is true that one's bones are under a covering of flesh, but what are regarded as the seats of feeling and thought, and are furthest down or inside, are not bones, but the heart, within the ribs, and the brain, inside the skull.

Shakespeare has 'I feel't upon my bones' (*Timon of Athens*, III, vi).

339

fifty-fifty. *fifty per cent to A, and fifty to B; half and half; halves; equal shares.* The expression is used with reference to circumstances in which two amounts or numbers in a computation are equal. Presumably **fifty-fifty** has been chosen and not e.g. 'forty-forty', 'ten-ten', etc., to show not only that the two amounts or numbers are equal, but that, taken together, they constitute the total concerned.

340

fight shy. *carefully avoid having anything to do with a person or affair.* The collocation of 'fight' and 'shyness' seems contradictory. Perhaps 'fight' was introduced into the phrase to imply that a person makes violent exertions in trying to avoid a person or situation. But see Preface, p. ix, for Pearsall Smith's explanation of what seems to him in some idioms deliberate irrationality.

341

fight with one's back to the wall. *in a contention, private* *or public, make a final desperate struggle.* The allusion is to a person who in literal combat having been forced back on to a wall, and being unable, even if he wished, to retreat any further, must beat his opponent or be killed.

342

burn one's fingers: see 107.

343

have a finger in the pie. *be concerned in an affair.* 'in the pie' is an ellipsis for 'in making the pie'.

344

slip through one's fingers. The phrase is used with reference to a benefit, advantage, prospect of advancement or wealth, etc., that by carelessness one lets escape by not seizing it.

345

snap one's fingers. *treat with contempt, as of no importance.* The gesture is cited by *S.O.E.D.* as having been, as far back as 1742, a sign of delight or of contempt; but today, when it is made, and when the phrase is used, the implication is only of contempt.

346

at the first blush. literally, *when first looked at;* figuratively *when first thought of* or *considered.* An early meaning of 'blush', now obsolete, is 'look', 'appearance'.

347

a fish out of water. *a person situated uncomfortably outside his usual or proper environment*, professionally, in business, socially, etc. The metaphor is as old as Chaucer.

348

a kettle of fish. The expression is always used with an ironic epithet, especially 'pretty', to mean *a plight, a disagreeable or awkward state of things.* It has been conjectured that a 'kettle of fish' used in this sense referred to one cooked in rather primitive conditions in the open air at a picnic or boating excursion. A kettle was not formerly confined to a covered vessel with a spout.

349

neither fish, flesh, fowl, nor good red herring. (The older form of this was without 'fowl'.) *neither one thing nor the other; unable to be classified.* The phrase can be applied to people or things. It appears as far back as in Udall's *Ralph Roister Doister* (printed 1566).

350

other fish to fry. *other matters to be engaged in that will be more interesting or profitable.* The phrase is recorded in use by John Evelyn as far back as 1660.

351

to cry stinking fish: see 178.

352

to drink like a fish: see 264.

353

to fish in troubled waters. *to try to benefit from other people's troubles.*

354

flash in the pan. *sudden display of what seems effective* *action, success, etc., which, however, is only transitory.* The phrase comes from the old flint-lock gun. The 'pan' was the place where a small quantity of gunpowder was exploded to ignite the charge in the barrel. If it failed to do this, there was only a 'flash' in the 'pan'.

355

That's flat (or **And that's flat**). *I mean it: let there be no doubt about it.* 'flat' here has the sense of 'unqualified', 'plain', 'downright'. Compare 'flat refusal', 'flat lie', 'flat denial', 'flat nonsense'.

356

a flea in his ear. The phrase is always used with reference to the peremptory dismissal of a person in circumstances, especially of unpleasant news, that will cause him acute vexation. The metaphor goes back in England to the sixteenth century, and is to be found even in ancient Greek. A Greek story says that when Croesus, King of Lydia, demanded tribute from the island of Samos, the Samians, influenced by Aesop, the fabulist, decided they would refuse, though that would risk war with Croesus, and sent his ambassador back 'with a flea in his ear'.

357

a flea-bite. *a matter of trifling, negligible inconvenience, annoyance, expense, etc., not worth giving serious thought to.*

358

flesh is heir to. *human beings are subject to.* This expression comes from *Hamlet*, III, i, 63. It is always quoted with reference to the troubles of life ('natural shocks' is Hamlet's term). 'flesh' here is, as defined by *S.O.E.D.*, 'human nature with its corporeal necessities and limitations'. 'heir to' = 'inherits', with probably an allusion to the sufferings that man inherits from Adam as a result of God's punishment for his transgression in Paradise.

359

flutter the dovecotes. literally, *cause a fluttering of the wings among the doves* (pigeons) *in their dovecote* (house for roosting and breeding); figuratively, *disturb the equanimity of a body of people.* The phrase comes from *Coriolanus*, V, v, 115:

like an eagle in a dove-cote, I
Flutter'd your Volscians in Corioli.

360

the fly in the ointment. *the one circumstance that, though trifling, ruins what otherwise would be perfect.* The phrase comes from the Bible (*Ecclesiastes*, 10, 1): 'Dead flies cause the ointment of the apothecary to send forth a stinking savour'.

361

a fool's errand. *a journey, or figuratively an enterprise, that is bound to be a failure.* The person undertaking the journey or enterprise may not be a fool, but the journey or enterprise is a foolish one.

362

fall on one's feet: see 325.

363

have cold feet: see 151.

364

have the ball at one's feet: see 33.

365

not let the grass grow under one's feet. *act promptly in starting on something one contemplates doing.*

366

put one's foot down. *be firm* (there is another idiom: 'take a firm stand') *in not allowing something, not agreeing to something.* Literally one puts one's foot down to stamp on a thing and destroy it.

367

put one's foot in it. *commit a blunder; do or say something that gets one into trouble, or causes disturbance, dismay, etc.* The metaphor is probably that of a person, walking along a road, who without noticing blunderingly steps into a mess.

368

set on foot. *start, initiate* (a scheme, business, etc.). There is personification of the scheme, etc., which is regarded as being placed on its feet, in a position in which it can make progress. Compare the application of the phrase to 'setting a man on his feet', meaning to start him on a career in business, etc.

369

shake the dust from one's feet. *leave a place, without regret, or with relief, or, generally, in anger or disgust.* The expression comes from a passage in the Bible, where Jesus says to the disciples 'And whosoever will not receive you, when you go out of that city, shake off the very dust from your feet for a testimony against them' (*Luke*, ix, 5). *Matthew* has 'of your feet'; *Mark*, 'under your feet'.

370

stand on one's own feet (or **legs**). *owe one's position to one's own efforts*, and not be dependent on others' help. 'own' is only an emphasiser, because one cannot stand on another's feet. The literal meaning therefore is that you are standing firm and well-balanced from your own poise, and not because you are supported by or leaning against somebody or something.

371

step off on the wrong foot. *in a project make an initial mistake.* The metaphor is from military drill. If in a given exercise the rule is to begin by moving the left foot forward, and a soldier moves the right, or vice versa, he is out of step with the rest of the soldiers.

372

foot the bill. literally, *sign one's name at the bottom of a written account:* e.g. for a meal at a hotel where one is staying; figuratively, *undertake responsibility for, or pay, a bill.*

373

a forlorn hope. *a hope that is most unlikely to be fulfilled; a desperate enterprise that is most unlikely to succeed.* Originally the phrase was an anglicised form of the Dutch words *verloren hoop* (of which *hoop* has no connection with the English word 'hope'), meaning literally a 'lost troop': a picked body of men, detached to the front to begin an attack. Brewer quotes Cromwell: 'our forlorn of horse marched within a mile of the enemy'.

374

forty winks. *a short sleep.* The expression, if analysed, is a strange one, in the use of the number 'forty'. The primary meaning of 'wink', now rare except in this phrase and in 'not a wink of sleep', is a closing of the eyes for sleep; but in the meaning with which 'forty winks' is used the implication is that one has only a few winks, whereas 'forty' was formerly used indefinitely to mean, not a small, but a large, number.

375

free lance. *person who acts independently* without being attached to an organisation or employer. In one of its meanings it applies to a person who is not attached to a political party. In another meaning it applies to a journalist who is not attached to a particular paper. In a more general meaning it applies to a person who, not being a member of a firm, organisation, etc., in receipt of a regular salary, is free to choose what work he will do and where he will from time to time offer his services.

'lance' was used early in the seventeenth century for a horse-soldier armed with a lance (i.e. as a synonym of 'lancer') or as a man at arms with his attendant retinue; but the present use of 'free lance', *S.O.E.D.* points out, is a figurative extension of the term as used by nineteenth-century writers to denote one of those military adventurers who in the Middle Ages offered their services as mercenaries, or with a view to plunder, to belligerent states.

376

friend at court. *person in an influential position who is, or if necessary could be, of valuable help to one.*

377

That is his (or **her** or **their**) **funeral.** *He is responsible for what has gone wrong and must bear the brunt of it.* The loss, disaster, or whatever it is, that has happened is personified as a person who has come to his death and is being buried, and the cost of whose funeral must be paid for by the person responsible for the death.

378

gall and wormwood. *bitter dissatisfaction and rancour.* 'gall', in its primary sense a secretion of the liver, became used as the type of an intensely bitter substance, and then figuratively for bitterness of spirit and rancour, supposed at one time to have their seat in the gall-bladder. 'wormwood' (a Middle English word, of which the origin is obscure, altered from the Old English word *wermod*, which is connected with 'vermouth') is primarily a plant, *artemisia*, proverbial for its bitter taste; later, in the sixteenth century, it became an emblem of what was bitter and grievous to the soul.

A combination of the two words appears in the Bible: 'remembering mine affliction and my misery, the wormwood and the gall' (*Lamentations*, 3, 19).

379

a game leg. *a lame or in other ways defective leg.* Wright's *English Dialect Dictionary* says that the adjective 'game' here was a dialectal and colloquial word meaning 'lame', 'crooked', 'deformed', 'injured': a form of 'gammy', and probably connected with an old French word *gambi* = 'bent', 'crooked'.

GAMES

380

scratch team, crew, etc. *set of people to take part in an activity (especially a competitive game) gathered together hastily*, when more careful selection of the best has not been possible. How 'scratch' came to have this meaning is not clear.

381

play fair is a colloquial synonym of **play the game** (383).

382

play a person false. *deceive, betray, a person.* This is another figurative extension of 'play', as in 'play the game' and 'play fair'. The words, if analysed, are equivalent to an elision of 'play the game with a person falsely': i.e. not keep to the rules. This figurative use of play is common: of acting a part, not on the stage, but in real life, as e.g. in 'play the man', 'play truant'.

383

play the game. *play the game fairly; act straightforwardly.* This idiom is an extension to conduct in general of the principles followed by people who take part in games, where 'to play the game' means to keep to the rules, to play it fairly. Compare **That's not cricket.**

384

The die is cast. *The decision is made; the course of action is irrevocably taken.* The metaphor comes from games of chance. 'die' is the singular of 'dice', but is not often used except in this phrase.

Slave! I have set my life upon a card,
And I will stand the hazard of the die.
Richard III, V, iv, 10.

385

The game is not worth the candle. *The result will not make the effort worth while.* The phrase is always used negatively. Brewer says the allusion is to a card-game in which the winnings will not pay the cost even of the candle used to light the players.

386

The game is up. The phrase is generally used with reference to a disreputable course of action that has been found out and must be abandoned.

387

within an ace. A thing is said to have been within an ace of happening, or a person to have been within an ace of doing or experiencing something, when it almost happened or he almost did or experienced it. A meaning of 'ace' in rackets is one point, or a service beating an opponent. The allusion may be to a person who, if he had gained one more point, would have won the game. Compare **by** (or **within**) **a hair's breadth** (465).

388

above (or **open and above**) **board.** *straightforward; without concealment*. Dr. Johnson in his Dictionary defined the term as 'In open sight; without artifice or trick. A figurative expression, borrowed from gamesters, who, when they put their hands under the table, are changing their cards.'

389

call a man's bluff. *unmask a person's pretence or deception.* This is a metaphor from the game of poker, where to 'bluff' is to try to impose on one's opponent by staking on a bad hand.

390

a clean sweep: see 138.

391

to follow suit. *to conform one's action to that of someone* *else*. The allusion is to card-playing, when one plays a card from the same suit as has been led.

392

have a card up one's sleeve. *have a resource in reserve to be used if necessary to strengthen one's position against opposition.* The allusion is to cardsharping.

393

a house of cards. *an insecure arrangement.* The term is an allusion to a children's game of constructing a toy house with playing-cards.

394

is on the cards. *possibly may happen.* The origin is probably fortune-telling by cards.

395

leave in the lurch. *abandon (a friend) when he is in difficulties.* The metaphor comes from card-games where 'lurch' is a state of score in which the loser is far below the winner. 'lurch' is derived from 'lourche', a French game like backgammon.

396

pass the buck to. (S) (1) *shift responsibility to, make a scapegoat of.* A 'buck' from which this sense comes is an article placed as a reminder before a poker-player whose turn it is to deal. The derivation of the word so used is unknown. (2) *tell the tale to, tell a tall tale to, try boasting talk on.* In this sense 'buck' is a Hindi word, meaning 'conversation', especially 'boasting talk'.

397

play fast and loose. *act in an unreliable and inconstant way.* The phrase is used most commonly with reference to relations between men and women in love affairs. If one took the phrase word by word, 'fast' might seem to mean 'in a fastened, fixed, attached way', at one moment (compare 'fast friends'; and 'hard and fast': see 484); and 'loose' to mean 'in an unfixed lax way', at another moment; but *S.O.E.D.* says that 'fast and loose' was the name of an old cheating game, and that as far back as the middle of the sixteenth century the phrase was used figuratively to mean 'slippery and inconstant'.

398

play one's cards well. *carry out a scheme adroitly and successfully.*

399

put one's cards on the table. *in negotiation and bargaining reveal candidly all one aims at gaining and be ready to concede.* The metaphor is from card-playing where in some games in some circumstances a player exposes his hand by showing on the table the cards he holds. Compare **above board** (388).

400

show one's hand. *show one's intentions.* The metaphor is from card-playing, in which the cards one has are called one's 'hand'.

401

sweep the board. *defeat everybody in a competition or contest.* A conjecture is that the allusion is to draughts where in one move a player can take every opposing piece off the board. Another conjecture is that it may refer to roulette, where, when zero comes up, and all stakes except those on zero are forfeited to the bank, the croupier sweeps the board of all the counters and money staked.

402

throw in one's hand. *give up, withdraw from a contest.* The metaphor is from card-playing, especially poker.

403

turn the tables. *reverse the position.* The expression is generally used with reference to A's altering his situation in relation to B with the result that he gets the better of him. Thus some prisoners succeed in overcoming their guards, whom they imprison. The former guards now 'have had the tables turned' on them. So too a person 'turns the tables' when he deals with a charge made against him by bringing a counter-charge. *C.O.D.* says the allusion is to the sense of the word 'tables' in the game of backgammon.

The five following words and phrases are figurative extensions of the meaning of a trump card in a suit that temporarily ranks above the others.

404

a trump. *a good fellow.*

405

a trump card. *one's most important resource in negotiations etc.*

406

play a, or one's last, trump card. *use one's most effective resource, help, expedient.*

407

trump up. invent, fabricate. *C.O.D.* for a meaning of the verb gives *defeat (a card) with a trump, play a trump,* but the connection between these and **trump up** is obscure.

408

turn up trumps. (of a person) *prove, sometimes unexpectedly, friendly and helpful;* (of an action) *prove satisfactory and advantageous.* 'trump' (singular), meaning 'a good fellow', is obsolescent.

409

below the belt. (1) *unfair* or (according to the construction in the context) (2) *unfairly.* (1) 'That hit was below the belt'; (2) 'That hit him below the belt'. The metaphor is from boxing, where a pugilist must not hit his opponent below the belt worn round the waist.

410

(1) come up, (2) bring up, to scratch. (1) *reach,* (2) *cause a person to reach, a decision that results in doing something.* The metaphor is here based on the noun 'scratch' in its meaning of the line in the prize ring marked (originally 'scratched') that pugilists used to toe at the beginning of a boxing-match.

411

play for safety. *make safety, and the avoidance of risks, the first consideration.* For 'play' see **play one's cards well** (398). The phrase comes from the game of bowls, where it is used for what a player does when, having no hope of a scoring shot, he tries to place the 'woods' (the wooden balls) in such a position that his opponent cannot score from them. One 'plays for safety' also in billiards by so placing one's own white ball that it is difficult, or impossible, for one's opponent to score from it.

412

There's the rub. *That is where doubt or difficulty enters.* This is a quotation from Hamlet's celebrated speech beginning 'To be or not to be' (*Hamlet*, III, i). Hamlet begins by approving suicide as an escape from the troubles of life, but then reflects that in another world we may be flying to fresh ills. In this passage 'rub' means 'impediment', and comes from the game of bowls, where it is the word used for an 'impediment' to the course of the bowls ('the woods'). As slang of today would put it: 'There's the snag.'

413

from pillar to post. The phrase is generally used with the past tense or past participle of the verb 'to drive': 'driven from pillar to post'. It means literally *from one place to another*; figuratively (and more usually) *from one resource to another:* in both uses with the implication of being harassed or repulsed.

Brewer says the phrase, which was originally 'from post to pillar', came from the tennis court, in allusion to the banging about of balls. The phrase was used in the fifteenth century by Lydgate for a person 'made to dance from whipping-post to pillory'.

414

have the ball at one's feet: see 33.

415

keep the ball rolling. *arrange that a conversation, discussion, enterprise, etc., shall continue.* The metaphor is from a ball-game, where play causes the ball to be kept in motion.

416

knuckle under; knuckle down. *submit, give in.* The primary meaning of the verb 'knuckle' (usually 'knuckle down') is to place one's knuckles on the ground in playing marbles. The connection between this and the figurative meaning of the phrase is obscure.

417

on one's toes. *in expectant readiness.* The allusion is to the start of a running race, when the competitors bend down in a position in which their feet are pushed forward on to their toes, ready to leap forward directly the signal is given.

418

toe the line; toe the mark. *do exactly what one is told; follow instructions in the smallest particular.* The metaphors come from athletics, where competitors about to take part in a race stand with their feet just touching a line. Compare **sign on the dotted line** (809).

419

a gay Lothario. *a man who goes about irresponsibly making love to women.* A character of that description, called Lothario, and mentioned as 'that haughty, gallant, gay Lothario', appears in *The Fair Penitent*, a tragedy by Nicholas Rowe (1678–1718).

420

get (or put) a person's back up: see 246.

421

get cracking. (S) *start hurrying, get busy, get going.* The allusion is to cracking a whip over a horse's back to make him move fast or to muster cattle.

422

get down to bedrock. *consider fundamental, essential, facts.* The phrase is generally used, in discussion or argument, for turning from superficial or unimportant details to fundamental principles. 'bedrock' is primarily a geological term for the solid rock underlying superficial formations, and so figuratively the 'bottom' or 'lowest level'. Compare **come (or get) down to brass tacks** (166).

423

get it in the neck. (S) *suffer a serious blow to one's undertakings, plans, etc., or be subjected to a vigorous verbal attack.* Compare **straight from the shoulder** (885).

424

get no change out of a person. *fail to get the information one hopes for.* (OO)

425

get one's goat. (S) *rouse, or become roused to, anger.* The allusion is unknown. One conjecture is that, as a goat, when annoyed, retaliates by butting the person who has offended it, so 'get one's goat' means to incite in one the spirit of an angry goat. Compare the next article: **get one's monkey up.**

426

get one's monkey up. This means the same as **get one's goat** (see the last article), and probably its origin is similar: the idea that something a person says or does excites the spirit of a monkey roused to retaliate by clawing and biting.

427

get the hang of. The expression is generally used negatively: 'I cannot get the hang of it'. *become familiar with the handling of a tool or the working of a machine;* or, of abstract things, *understand a situation, scheme, story, etc.;* or (an Americanism) *acquire the knack of (doing something).* *S.O.E.D.* cites, from the end of the eighteenth century, the use of 'hang' in the sense of 'the mode in which a thing hangs or is posed'. That is the nearest, but not a close, connection between the word 'hang' in the phrase and the current figurative meanings.

428

got out of bed on the wrong side. The expression is always preceded by 'He (or somebody) must have' (done so) with reference to a person who has evidently started the day in a bad humour. There is no right or wrong side for getting out of bed except that one may be nearer to, say, the dressing-table or wash-hand-basin; and the statement is always made as an ironical suggestion that nothing less serious than such an experience could account for the irrational bad temper, peevishness, fault-finding, etc., that the person concerned is showing.

429

(1) **get,** (2) **have, the wind up.** (S) (1) *become,* (2) *be scared.* Pearsall Smith has told us that a notable number of our idioms are of nautical origin, and 'the wind up' might

suggest that this expression had something to do with bad weather that caused anxiety to a sailor. I have learnt, however, from an expert yachtsman that it is not nautical, and that, less romantically, 'wind' refers to the flatulence some people suffer from when they are nervous.

430

get wind of. *hear rumours about* (something that is happening or about or likely to happen). The allusion is to the smell conveyed by the wind that indicates to animals the whereabouts or existence of a thing.

431

gild the pill. *make an unpleasant thing appear less so; soften down an unpleasant necessity*, by action or by words. Pills used to be coated with a thin layer of gold leaf to make them less offensive to sight or taste.

432

gird (or **gird up**) **one's loins.** *summon strength of will to enter vigorously on an enterprise.* Literally the phrase means to encircle the waist with a belt. It is biblical. Mr. Eric Partridge in his *Dictionary of Clichés* cites four passages in the Old Testament where the expression is used literally, and in the New Testament (I *Peter* 1, 13) a figurative use: 'Wherefore gird up the loins of your mind'.

433

give a handle: i.e. give something by which a thing may be (figuratively) taken hold of: so *give an excuse, a pretext, grounds.*

434

give a leg up. *help a person*, especially in a difficulty.

The metaphor comes from helping a person to mount a horse.

435

give a person the cold shoulder. *ignore a person, or cut him, or treat him with noticeable disrespect.* Pearsall Smith says the expression probably meant to put a cold shoulder of mutton before an unhonoured guest. A friend suggests that, more simply, it is a figurative extension of the action of turning one's back, including one's shoulder, on a person. 'cold' is often used with reference to treating a person in a distant and ungenial way.

436

give a wide berth to. *carefully avoid, keep as far away as possible from,* a person, conditions, etc. Literally 'berth' is a nautical term for 'convenient sea-room' for a ship to move, or to swing at anchor, or to be moored at a wharf.

437

give chapter and verse. *cite the precise reference for a statement.* The phrase was originally used for references to the Bible. Isaac Disraeli (father of the statesman) in his *Curiosities of Literature* writes: 'The proverbial expression of "chapter and verse" seems peculiar to ourselves, and I suspect originated in the Puritanic period, from the frequent use of appealing to the Bible on the most frivolous occasions by those whom South (a court preacher in the reign of Charles II) calls "those men at chapter and verse".'

438

to give the devil his due: see 235.

439

go at it hammer and tongs. *engage in an undertaking or* *quarrel with great energy.* The allusion is to the tools used by a blacksmith.

440

go back on. The metaphor is that of a person who advances, with the intention of doing, or as if to do, something, and then, turning back, does not do it. With reference to a person it means to be 'disloyal', 'treacherous'. With reference to one's word, promise, etc., it means 'break', and, to an engagement, 'withdraw from', in which sense, followed by 'on', 'upon', and at one time 'of', it was used as early as the sixteenth century.

441

go by the board. *be abandoned, be dropped:* usually with reference to schemes, arrangements, etc. Primarily the phrase meant 'fall overboard'. One of the meanings of 'board' used to be a 'ship's side'. This meaning still survives in the term 'freeboard': a ship's side above the water-line.

442

go off the deep end: see 282.

443

go one better. (absolutely) *do better* (than he or that). Perhaps the original allusion was to games where the competitors were given marks.

444

go out of one's way. *take special trouble*, especially when this means doing something that will cause one to depart from the ordinary course of one's activities.

445

go over the ground. *examine the circumstances.*

446

go the whole hog. *do the thing thoroughly.* (OO)

447

go through fire and water. *endure extreme difficulties, dangers, sufferings.* The risk of being burnt or drowned is used as emblematic of what a person is ready to undergo or has undergone. Brewer says the expression may allude to the medieval ordeal by fire and water in trials in Anglo-Saxon times. The phrase appears in a translation of Xenophon's *Oeconomicus* in 1534. Shakespeare uses it in *The Merry Wives of Windsor*, III, iv. Mr. Eric Partridge says it became a cliché about the middle of the last century.

448

go through thick and thin. This means the same as **go through fire and water** (see the last article), though it does not usually imply such an extreme degree of danger. The allusion is to travelling in country that in some parts is only sparsely wooded, and therefore means easy going, but where in others one has to make one's way with difficulty through low trees and bushes growing densely together.

Chaucer uses the phrase literally in *The Reeve's Tale* (144): 'he ginneth gon toward the fen . . . thurgh thikke and thurgh thenne'. The earliest record given by the *Oxford Book of English Proverbs* for a figurative use is in 1543, by Richard Grafton: 'Kyng Richard purposed to goo thorow thicke and thinne in this matter'.

449

go to one's head. *make one excited; intoxicate one* (in which sense it can be used also with reference to alcoholic intoxication).

The phrase connotes a mental state less out of control than **turn one's head** (see 505).

450

go to pot. (S) (1) *seriously deteriorate;* (2) *go to ruin, or be destroyed.* The metaphor is that of meat, not good enough for other purposes, being cut up into pieces, to be thrown into the pot, a 'stock-pot' on the fire, into which various things, and odds and ends, are put, in order to make a stock-pot; but the connection between this and the current meanings of the phrase is not close.

451

go to the dogs: see 242.

452

go to the wall. (in a struggle, competition, etc.) *get the worst of it, have to give way or succumb.* The allusion is to a person walking along a street, or to a rider or carriage folk, pushing aside, towards the wall, somebody who is overtaken and passed. There is a proverb 'The weakest goes to the wall'. On the other hand there is an expression 'give a person the wall', which means to let him walk next to it as the cleaner and safer.

453

go west: see 222.

454

goes without saying. (The phrase is usually preceded by 'It', followed by a 'that' clause.) *need not be said, mentioned, pointed out.* Why then say it, etc.? At best the phrase is equivalent to 'of course', but that is no defence, for 'of course' is itself so overworked that in most contexts it is mere padding.

A corresponding absurdity is the statement 'I need not say', by a person who in the next breath goes on to say it.

455

touch and go. *an extremely narrow escape from failure, disaster, etc.; a close thing.* Brewer says it may be a metaphor from driving, when one vehicle touches another, passing it, without injury. Pearsall Smith says that the phrase may come from a nautical use for a ship touching rocks or the ground with her keel, and then sailing on without damage.

456

in one's good books: see 79.

457

put a good face on: see 311.

458

throw good money after bad. *having had an unprofitable enterprise, waste money that will add to the monetary loss:* that is to say, spend money that is now 'good' (= 'safe') but will very likely become a further loss. Compare, for the contrary action, **cut one's losses** (194).

459

against the grain. *contrary to one's natural inclination.* One of the meanings of 'grain' is the arrangement of the constituent particles in flesh, wood, stone, etc. In 'against the grain' the reference is probably to wood, which is harder to cut across the grain.

460

grasp the nettle. *by acting with courageous determination suffer less than if one does nothing or takes only mild measures.* One is more likely to be stung if one handles a nettle gently than if one grasps it firmly. (Lyly's *Euphues* 1579.)

461

a grass widow. *a wife temporarily living apart from her husband* (who e.g. may be abroad), *or on holiday:* like a horse 'out at grass', not doing its normal work.

462

the Greek Kalends. This is a jocularity for *never.* The Kalends was the name of the first day of the month in the Roman calendar, but the ancient Greeks had no such date.

463

the green-eyed monster. *jealousy.* From *Othello*, III, i, 165:

> O ! beware my Lord, of jealousy;
> It is the green-eyed monster which doth mock
> The meat it feeds on.

464

up a gum-tree. *in almost inextricable difficulties.* 'Gum-trees' (the eucalyptus) grow to an immense height. One species reaches 480 feet (the tallest known tree). Perhaps the figurative meaning of the expression is based on the idea that, if one were high up in a tree of this sort, it would be extremely difficult to get down, especially as it has a smooth trunk and no branches near the ground.

465

by (or within) a hair's breadth (or hairbreadth). *barely,* *narrowly, only just.* There is also the adjective 'hair-breadth'; 'He had a hairbreadth escape'. The breadth of a human hair is about one fiftieth of an inch.

Compare **within an ace** (387).

466

make one's hair stand on end: see 284.

467

not turn a hair. *not show signs of being affected, disturbed, excited, etc.* The allusion, says *S.O.E.D.*, is to a horse not showing, by a roughening of the hair, that it is sweating.

Compare **keep one's hair on** with the same meaning; and **lose one's hair** = *get angry.*

468

to a hair. *exactly, to a nicety.* See **by** (or **within**) **a hair's breadth** (465). Compare also **to a T** (898).

469

to split hairs. in argument *to draw over-fine distinctions, or in negotiation to dispute over extremely petty points.*

470

cap in hand: see 117.

471

from hand to mouth. *without regular means of subsistence.* The image seems t) be that of a person whose meals are so uncertain that the minute he has any food he must at once put it into his mouth.

472

hand in (or **and**) **glove.** (*be*) *on intimate terms, in intimate* *relations,* especially with reference to a plan, business transaction, etc.: i.e. as closely connected as a glove is to the hand that wears it. The expression appears first, in English, in John Florio's translation of Montaigne's essays in 1603. Otherwise the earliest record of the phrase is in 1680, in R. Mansel's *Narrative of the Popish Plot:* 'Mrs. Collier, to whom Mr. Willoughby was such a crony that they were hand in glove'.

473

have the whip hand. *control.* Literally the phrase means that one has in one's hand a whip with which to control another. There is in the phrase an implication that the control is exercised rather harshly. The use of the expression goes back to 1583.

474

put one's hand to the plough. *set about undertaking an important and difficult task.* The phrase is an echo of a passage in the Bible (*Luke*, ix, 62): 'No man, having put his hand to the plough, and looking back, is fit for the kingdom of God'.

475

show one's hand: see 400.

476

wash one's hands. *divest oneself of any further connection with or responsibility for a matter or person.* The phrase comes from the description in the Bible of Pontius Pilate's washing his hands at the trial of Jesus (*Matthew*, 26, 24).

477

get the hang of: see 427.

478

hang by a thread. *depend for its continuance on extremely fragile conditions.* The phrase is used especially of the life of a person who is so seriously ill, or of the fate of a person that is so precarious, that the life or the fate is regarded as being suspended by a thread that may break at any moment. The allusion may have been originally to the sword of Damocles. Dionysius the Elder, King of Syracuse (4th century B.C.), invited one of his courtiers, Damocles, to a banquet where a sword was suspended over his head by a single horse-hair, as a symbol of the precarious fortunes of the great.

479

hang fire. *not produce the result expected when expected.* The failure to do this may be only temporary. The allusion is to a firearm that does not go off. *S.O.E.D.* mentions a use of 'hang' in the sense of 'be or remain in dubious suspense'.

480

hang on by one's eyelids (or **eyelashes** or **eyebrows**). *manage to keep oneself in a precarious situation.* The situation may be a physical one: e.g. a narrow ledge on a mountain; or a figurative one: e.g. in civilian employment.

The person is imagined as being suspended from the object to which he is clinging, and being attached to this only by his eyelids etc.

481

hang in the balance. An event is said to 'hang in the balance' when the probability of its happening or not happening seems equal: i.e. when it leaves one in a state of

dubious suspense. The metaphor is that of a weighing machine, in which either pan may tip up or down.
Compare the next article.

482

hang in the wind, like **hang in the balance** (see the last article), is an expression used about something that may or may not happen, but here the allusion is nautical, and is to the uncertain, hesitating course a sailing ship sometimes seems to take when the wind is variable.

483

hang on like grim death: see 223.

484

hard and fast. *subject to no exception or modification; immutable.* The phrase is generally used with reference to rules, principles, opinions. It is a figurative extension of 'hard' = 'firm', 'firmly fixed'; and of 'fast' = 'fastened'. The words generally qualify 'line' or 'rule'. In origin the phrase is nautical, and is used of a boat or ship that has run aground.

485

has had it. (S) The phrase, which originated in the First World War, was first used to mean that a soldier had been killed. It was later extended in a general sense, and loosely, to a person who by misfortune was irretrievably 'done for', or who by his own fault had irretrievably 'done for himself'.
A classical friend draws my attention to the cry *Habet* (Latin) = 'He has it', by the spectators at Roman gladiatorial contests when a gladiator was struck.

486

the hat trick. This is a cricket phrase for *taking three wickets with three successive balls.* It is sometimes used outside cricket with reference to a *triple success.*

In the early days of cricket the players used to wear top hats, and Brewer says that a bowler performing the feat was entitled to a new hat at the expense of his club. Another explanation that has been given is that the captain used to take round a hat and each member of the team would put a shilling in it.

487

haul over the coals. *find serious fault with; call to account.* The allusion is to the treatment of heretics in the Middle Ages. Thus kings and barons would demand money from Jews, and, if they resisted, would have them dragged over the coals of a slow fire until they consented to give what was asked. Brewer mentions Front-de-Boeuf in Scott's *Ivanhoe* as threatening to have this done to Isaac.

It is probably a tendency to alliteration that has led to the variant 'call over the coals'.

488

haul up. (1) *reprove.* 'The teacher hauled him up for using such a slang expression in an essay.' (2) *arrest and bring before a police magistrate.* The origin of 'haul up' is perhaps nautical. In that sense (but as an intransitive verb) it means to trim the sails of a ship so as to sail nearer to the wind.

489

bite a person's head off: see 58.

490

bury one's head in the sand: see 111.

491

go to one's head: see 449.

492

head over ears (or **head and ears** or **over head and ears**); or **heels** instead of **ears.** *deeply:* e.g. in love, in debt. The metaphor is that of a person immersed in water.

493

Heads I win, tails you lose. *However the matter goes, I am bound to benefit and you to lose:* i.e. it is a one-sided and utterly unfair arrangement. The reference is to the tossing of a coin to decide, according to the obverse or reverse falling uppermost, which of two alternatives is to be followed, with the exclamation 'Heads!' or 'Tails!' In *Hudibras* (1672) Samuel Butler has

> For matrimony, and hanging here,
> Both go by destiny so clear,
> That you as sure may pick and choose,
> As cross I win, and pile you lose.

'cross' was formerly used for the face of a coin, from the figure of a cross stamped upon it; and 'pile' for the reverse side.

494

heap coals of fire on a person's head. *make a person who has injured one feel remorse or shame by kindness, generosity, return of good for evil.* The phrase comes in the Bible: 'If thine enemy be hungry, give him bread to eat; and if he be thirsty, give him water to drink; for thou shalt heap coals of fire upon his head' (*Proverbs*, 25, 21; and there is a similar passage in *Romans*, 12, 20). It is found also in Langland's *Piers Plowman* (1377).

495

hit the nail (or **the right nail) on the head.** *guess right; come to the right conclusion; express the exact truth;* (to use another metaphor) *hit the mark.*

496

It is on your (or **your own) head. On your head be it.** (The words are generally uttered as a warning.) *It is you who will be responsible for any disaster that results, blame that is imputed, vengeance that falls.* The metaphor is as old as Homer.

497

keep one's head. *keep one's mental balance* (regarded as centred in one's brain). Contrast **lose one's head** (499).

498

keep one's head above water. *succeed in living within one's income:* that is to say (to keep to the metaphor), not to sink into and be submerged by money difficulties.

499

lose one's head. The opposite to **keep one's head** (497).

500

make head or tail of it. *understand it.* The phrase is generally used only negatively: e.g. 'I can't make head or tail of it'. Compare **make anything of it** (576). Mr. Eric Partridge in his *Dictionary of Clichés* gives a plural form: 'heads or tails'. Though the general meaning of the phrase is simple, the connection between that meaning and the face value of the words is obscure. Perhaps 'head or tail' stands merely for 'beginning or end', and the meaning is 'I cannot make it out from beginning to end'. A friend suggests the following explanation. 'The "it" is a number of circumstances, or a spoken description, without clear form, constituting a confused mass, like a shapeless creature in which one cannot make out which is the head and which the tail: i.e. figuratively, we cannot see a connected picture, or follow a sequence of thought.' Mr. Auty suggests that the allusion is to being unable to tell the difference between the head and tail of a much used coin.

501

off one's head. *out of one's senses, crazy.* The expression is generally used with reference to a person who has only temporarily lost control of his mental balance: e.g. from excitement. Thus a person can be said to be 'off his head for joy'.

The phrase if analysed is a strange one, because the natural image would be that of a person without a head (as containing the seat of reason in the brain): i.e. whose head was off him, rather than that he should be off his head. The person is regarded as carrying on his existence away, separated, removed, from, and so, figuratively, independent of, the element of reason seated in his brain.

Compare the slang expressions 'off one's nut' and 'off one's chump'.

502

put one's head in the lion's mouth. *take a great risk.* The allusion is to a person at a circus who performs this trick.

503

run one's head against a stone wall. *do something that is bound to be a failure, as it will come up against difficulties or* *opposition that cannot be overcome.* The metaphor is recorded as used as far back as the end of the sixteenth century.

504

talk a person's head off. *weary a person by too much talking.* Perhaps the idea was that the person nodded with weariness, so much that his head dropped off.

505

turn one's head. *cause one to lose one's mental balance.* The expression is used with reference to a person whose success or good fortune creates in him inflated ideas of his importance, merits, prospects, etc. Among the meanings of 'turn', *O.E.D.* gives 'cause to be giddy, swim, reel, turn in a whirl'. Such a sense of 'turn' goes back to Shakespeare, who, however, uses it intransitively (*King Lear*, IV, v): 'Lest my head turn'. Transitively Scott has, in *The Black Dwarf*, 'to turn the brain'; and Hughes, in *Tom Brown at Oxford*, 'turned the poor girl's head'.

506

heal the breach. *make up a quarrel.* 'breach' is connected with the word 'break'. Its figurative use for a state of ruptured relations goes back to the early part of the seventeenth century.

507

have one's heart in one's boots. *be dispirited, deeply depressed, timorously anxious, about something.* The heart, regarded as the seat of the emotions, is imagined as, instead of elevating and buoying one up from the upper regions of the breast, sinking deep down into the abdomen, and then lower still to the extremities of one's legs. Compare the phrases 'a sinking heart' and 'a heart like lead'.

The date of the earliest record of this expression, as given by the *Oxford Dictionary of English Proverbs*, is only about a hundred years ago. The expression, however, of having one's heart in one's 'shoes' goes back to the seventeenth century; in one's 'heels' to the sixteenth; in one's 'hose' to the fifteenth.

508

have one's heart in one's mouth. *be greatly alarmed by what is happening or is expected to happen at once.* There, as contrasted with the image of a heart that sinks, in the expression dealt with in the last article, it is thought of as jumping upward, and causing a disturbing, choking, sensation.

The date of the earliest record of this expression is cited by the *Oxford Dictionary of English Proverbs* as 1548, in a translation by Nicholas Udall of Erasmus's *Paraphrase of the New Testament*. The second record given is of its use by Addison some two centuries later.

509

He has his heart in the right place. *Though not without faults he has sound ideas and principles; he means well; the fundamental elements in his character are good.* Stevenson cites it as used first in 1809. The image on which the metaphor is based is obscure. That the heart has popularly been conceived to move about is shown by the proverbial phrases treated in the last two articles, and by many passages of poetry describing joy. But probably in the present expression the heart is conceived, not as an organ that shifts its position about the body, but, in one of the other senses it has, as the soul, the spirit, one's inmost thoughts and feelings, regarded as directed to worthy interests and aims.

510

warm the cockles of one's heart. *give a deep sense of satisfaction. S.O.E.D.* mentions, as one explanation that has been given of the phrase, the likeness of a heart to the shell of a cockle. 'cockles of one's heart' would therefore mean 'heart (hearts) of the heart'. Compare 'heart of heart(s)' in *Hamlet*, III, ii, and Wordsworth's Ode on Immortality, 189. Brewer says that 'cockles' is a popularised form of the Latin word *cochlea* in *cochlea cordis* = 'ventricles of the heart'.

As far back as 1671 there is a record of the expression 'rejoice the cockles of his heart'. In 1792 Sir Walter Scott wrote in a letter: 'would have delighted the very cockles of your heart'. To 'warm' them is recorded first as used by Captain Marryat in *Jacob Faithful*, 1834.

511

wear one's heart on one's sleeve. *expose, so that everyone knows, one's most intimate feelings.* The origin of the phrase is in a passage in *Othello*, I, i, 64, where Iago says:

> When my outward action doth demonstrate
> The native art and figure of my heart
> In compliment extern, 'tis not long after
> But I will wear my heart upon my sleeve
> For daws to peck at.

512

hide one's light under a bushel. *From modesty keep one's talents hidden.* The phrase comes from a passage in the Bible, where Christ says 'Neither do men light a candle, and put it under a bushel, but in a candlestick; and it giveth light unto all that are in the house' (*Matthew*, 5, 15): that is, they do not put it in a place where it will remain unseen.

513

highfaluting (or **highfalutin**). *pompous, bombastic* (speech or writing). The expression came from U.S.A. *O.E.D.* says that 'faluting' may have been a whimsical variant of 'fluting' (= 'playing the flute') or a grandiose equivalent of 'flying' or 'flown'.

514

hit it off. *agree; be congenial to one another.* The phrase can be used absolutely, but it is generally followed by 'together' or 'with one another'.

In the seventeenth century 'to hit' had a meaning *to agree.*

515

hit off. *imitate or parody to a nicety the behaviour of, or something said or written by, a person.* The figurative blows, hits, aimed at his characteristics are regarded as reaching their mark. There is a synonymous expression *to take off* a person or thing. The noun 'a hit' is currently used with the meaning of 'a success', as for example a popular play.

516

Hobson's choice. *the acceptance of what is offered when there is no alternative.* In the *Spectator* (No. 509: 14th October 1712) Steele gave an account of the origin of the phrase. Hobson, he said, was Tobias Hobson, who kept an inn at Cambridge and hired out horses. Though he had a large number of horses, he always insisted that a prospective hirer should take the one nearest the stable door: whence, said Steele, 'it became the proverb, when what ought to be your selection was forced on you, to say, "Hobson's choice"'.

It has been pointed out that Hobson's practice was sensible, because the horse nearest to the door was the one that had been longest in the stable since it was previously used, and so the most rested.

The *Dictionary of National Biography* has a page and a half about Hobson, who died in 1631: that is to say, eighty years before the publication of this account in the *Spectator*. He amassed a handsome fortune, and made bequests to Cambridge, in which a street is named after him; and Milton wrote two humorous epitaphs on him.

517

hocus-pocus. *humbug, nonsense*, applied especially to an imposition, pretence, swindle. *S.O.E.D.* says it was originally the name assumed by, or given to, a conjuror, being the first words of a sham Latin formula used by one in the seventeenth century. It was alleged to be a parody of *Hoc est corpus* ('This is the body') from the Mass. Later it came to mean a juggler's trick, and then cheating.

518

hoist with his own petard (often incorrectly 'on' instead of 'with'). *be defeated, or foiled, by the very means taken to injure others*. The medieval petard was an engine of war, charged with gunpowder, that was used for blowing in a gate or door, making a breach in a wall, etc. 'hoist' (past participle of 'hoise', an old form of 'hoist') = 'raised aloft', 'lifted up', 'blown up'. Shakespeare (*Hamlet*, III, iv) has ''tis the sport to have the enginer Hoist with his own petar'. Sometimes the men working this engine would be injured or even killed by it.

519

to hold the baby; to be left holding the baby. (S) have foisted on to one an unwanted, tiresome, troublesome, embarrassing task and responsibility.

520

hold water. The expression is generally used negatively, with reference to a scheme or argument that is regarded as not *sound or practicable.* The allusion is to a receptacle that leaks.

521

hole and corner. This is an adjectival phrase applied to conduct or a transaction that is *not open and straightforward*, but (to use another metaphor) underhand. The image may be that of a person who in his clandestine movements hides himself: indoors in dark corners, out-of-doors in holes in the ground. Cf. *Acts*, 26, 26: 'this thing was not done in a corner'.

522

by hook or by crook. *by any means, easy or hard*, or, sometimes, *honest or dishonest.* Brewer considers that the phrase comes from an old manorial custom that authorised tenants to take as much firewood from the hedges etc. as could be cut with a crook or bill-hook, and as much low timber as could be reached by a shepherd's crook.

523

the ins and outs. (1) *the details of an event, story, etc. C.O.D.* gives, as the primary meaning of the phrase, 'windings to and fro'; and *S.O.E.D.* 'windings or turnings in a road': the ramifications causing it at one point to diverge from a direct course, and then to bend back into the straight. The phrase is now generally used only figuratively, for the details of an event, story, argument, etc., or of a course of procedure; or with reference to the shifting fortunes of political parties in the House of Commons, where the Government represents the 'ins', and the Opposition the 'outs'.

524

The iron had entered into his soul. *He had become permanently embittered;* or *bitterness had entered deeply into his thoughts or feelings.* The phrase comes from the Prayer Book version of *Psalms,* 105, 18; but it is a mistranslation of the Hebrew of a phrase stating that 'his person entered into the iron': i.e. he was imprisoned in iron fetters; and the Authorised Version of the Bible has 'he was laid in iron', and the Revised Version 'he was laid in chains of iron'.

525

irons in the fire. *projects, plans, undertakings, on which one is engaged.* The phrase is often used with reference either to a person engaged in too many undertakings to be able to execute them satisfactorily, or to a person's having one or more expedients if the present undertaking fails. The metaphor is of articles in a blacksmith's forge.

526

a Job's comforter. *one who, affecting to sympathise with someone in trouble, aggravates his distress by saying that he brought it on himself.* The allusion is to the friends of Job who accused and reproached and exhorted him. 'Then Job answered and said "I have heard many such things: miserable comforters are ye all"' (*Job,* 16, 2).

527

jump from the frying-pan into the fire. *in trying to escape from one difficulty, trouble, etc., find oneself in as bad a position as before, or perhaps a worse one.* The idiom is useful, vigorous, and vivid, though analysis does not expose a close connection between the image and the current meaning unless one personifies something that is being cooked as wishing to escape from the frying-pan. The expression is found as far back as in John Heywood's collection of proverbs (1546).

528

It's just one of those things. This recent phrase is an elision of 'It's the sort of thing fate sends, for which nobody is to blame, and that a sensible person will accept with philosophic resignation'.

529

keep a stiff upper lip. *endure misfortune with firm courage.* If one is downhearted, there is a tendency for one's mouth to relax.

530

keep one's head: see 497.

531

keep one's head above water: see 498.

532

keep one's (or another's) nose down to the grindstone. with reference to oneself: *work incessantly;* with reference to another: *make work incessantly.* A grindstone is a thick revolving disk for grinding (sharpening or smoothing by friction), and in the metaphor the person operating this is regarded as being so close to it that his nose is almost touching it. The metaphor is recorded as in use as far back as 1539.

533

to keep the pot boiling. *to continue energetically to engage in work, producing money to support oneself with,* is the most general sense of the expression. It is sometimes used of a person practising an art: e.g. a writer, painter, musician, with reference to a particular work he is engaged in, but about which he has no illusions that it is of first-rate artistic value. Compare the term 'pot-boiler'.

534

a kettle of fish: see 348.

535

kick one's heels. *be unoccupied, or kept waiting, and to be annoyed because of that.* The metaphor is that of shuffling one's feet aimlessly instead of using them in moving about with some set purpose. Compare **twiddle one's thumbs** (972).

536

kick over the traces. *become insubordinate, by rebelling against people who have authority over one, or breaking disciplinary rules.* The metaphor is taken from driving. The action of the person concerned is described as if it were that of a horse breaking away from the traces (the two side-straps or chains by which a horse draws a vehicle).

537

kill the goose that lays the golden eggs. *do something that, designed to produce more benefits from a certain source, destroys the source and leaves one without any benefits.* The allusion is to a fable of Aesop in which a man, having a goose that laid a golden egg every day, cut it open to get what he imagined would be a large number of eggs, to find that all he had was a dead bird.

538

kill two birds with one stone. *with one action accomplish* *two different purposes.* The expression is used figuratively as far back as by Thomas Hobbes, in 1656, but it appears first in R. Cotgrave's French-English Dictionary in 1611, as a translation of the French phrase: *d'une pierre faire deux coups.*

539

a King Charles's head: in such a sentence as '**It is a King Charles's head with him**'. *an obsession.* The allusion is to Mr. Dick, a half-witted character in *David Copperfield*, who was composing a 'Memorial' about his life, 'which never made the least progress, for King Charles the First always strayed into it, sooner or later'.

540

knock into a cocked hat. *utterly defeat:* a person, in a contest; or an argument, theory, etc. The old triangular hat worn in the eighteenth century was formed from the Puritan round hat of the preceding century by turning up (or 'cocking') the brim. Hence 'to knock into a cocked hat' came to mean to change a thing drastically, and then, by extended implication, to defeat utterly.

541

I do not know him from Adam. *I should not recognise him.* 'Adam' here means 'any man': i.e. 'I could not identify one man as being this person rather than any other'.

542

know all the answers. *be well-informed, bright, and sharp:* often used rather ironically with reference to a person who, in slang, is called 'a know-all'.

543

know on which side one's bread is buttered. *know what course it will be politic to take, in one's relations with people, that will benefit one.* If an attempt is made to analyse the phrase the connection between the words and the figurative meaning is obscure. A slice of bread is not more palatable if buttered on one side rather than on the other. Moreover, when a slice of bread is eaten, it is bitten through equally on both sides. 'on which side' therefore seems not to refer to the slice but to mean 'in what circumstances' you will succeed in getting it buttered.

The earliest record of the phrase is by John Heywood in his book of proverbs that appeared in 1546.

A later proverb (of which the first record is in 1678) has 'His bread is buttered on both sides', meaning that he is situated in favourable circumstances all round.

544

know the ropes. *be conversant with the main principles and methods on which a business or other organisation is run, or an undertaking or transaction is carried on.* This is a nautical metaphor that alludes to the familiarity an experienced sailor has of the ropes, on a ship, for the various sails.

545

on its last legs. *near its end.* In its primary sense the expression refers to a material object of domestic use such as a chair or table, that is old and will not last much longer; in a secondary sense to an institution that is nearly defunct, a business that is near failure, etc. With 'his' substituted for 'its' it would refer to a person who is near death, in which sense there is a record of its use as far back as 1599, in a play by Massinger.

546

the last straw. *the final culminating circumstance that makes a situation unendurable.* The allusion is to the proverb 'It is the last straw that breaks the camel's back'.

547

laugh in (or **up**) **one's sleeve.** *laugh to oneself, be secretly amused.* The idiom no doubt came into use at a time when men wore pendent sleeves, which they could hold in front of their face to hide a smile. The figurative use of this expression appears as far back as 1506.

548

laugh on the wrong side of his mouth (or **on the other side of his face**): see 306.

549

(1) lay at a person's door; (2) lie at a person's door. (1) *place on a person responsibility for something that has happened.* This is a figurative extension of the fact that the tenant of a house is responsible for what happens in it or so near to it that it is at his door. (2) There is the corresponding idiom where the responsibility is the subject of the intransitive verb 'lie'.

550

lead a person up the garden (or **garden path**). *delude, lead astray, a person;* or *deceive him about one's intentions or wishes.* In this modern metaphor the inducing of a person, instead of remaining in security at home, to leave the house and wander about a garden is taken as symbolical of leading astray.

551

Least said, soonest mended. *If one wishes to heal a quarrel, the best course is to stop speaking about the point at issue.*

552

leave a person flat. *finish a discussion or argument by utterly defeating one's opponent.* The defeated person is metaphorically knocked down, laid out, and flattened. Stevenson cites its use in 1530.

553

leave no stone unturned. *take every possible means, spare no effort, in trying to accomplish an aim.* The origin of the phrase is said by Brewer to be a translation of the words uttered by the Oracle of Delphi to one Polycrates, a Theban, who in the fifth century B.C. asked how he was to find a treasure that a Persian general, defeated by the Greeks at the battle of Plataea, was rumoured to have buried on the battlefield. Mrs. J. E. Heseltine in the *Oxford Dictionary of English Proverbs* mentions, besides this alleged origin, two others that have been put forward. Liddell and Scott, the compilers of the celebrated Greek Lexicon, say that the phrase may have come from the game of draughts. The third suggestion is that the words of the Oracle of Delphi may have referred to fishermen turning over stones as they hunted for crabs.

The expression is used figuratively in English literature far back as 1550; in Greek by Euripides; in Latin by Pliny.

554

a left-handed compliment. *something said to, or written to or about, a person that, while affecting to praise, has an underlying implication that is unfavourable.* One ordinarily gives a present with the right hand. Here in this phrase a person is imagined to be doing so with the left hand, as more suitable for what is not genuinely a present. Compare the derivation of the English word 'sinister' from the Latin *sinister*, which means 'left'.

555

Let (or **Leave**) **well alone.** *Do not disturb a state of affairs that is fairly satisfactory, lest you make it worse rather than better.* Compare **Let sleeping dogs lie** (243).

556

lick into shape. *mould into desirable form.* The reference might be, e.g., to training a young person in manners, or in efficiency at work; or to revising some written work, etc. The allusion is to an animal that licks its young. There was a belief that bears did this to their newly born cubs in order to mould them into shape. The *Oxford Book of English Proverbs* cites a passage about this as far back as 1483, in a translation from the French of a book called *The Pilgrimage of the Soul* by G. Deguilaville. George Chapman in *The Widow's Tears* (1612) and Robert Burton in *The Anatomy of Melancholy* (1621) used the phrase figuratively.

557

If you don't like it, you can lump it. *If you don't like it, all you can do is to resign yourself and put up with it, however unwillingly.* This sense of 'lump' has no connection with any other senses of either the verb or the noun. *S.O.E.D.* describes it as being 'of symbolic sound: compare "dump", "hump", "mump"'. Mr. Ivor Brown in *I Break My Word* suggests, perhaps jokingly, that 'lump' is a sort of compound of 'look' and 'grumpy'. H. C. Wyld gives 'lumper' as a noun meaning 'labourer employed in loading and unloading vessels'. A friend tells me he remembers that when he was a boy, in Liverpool, 'lumper' was applied, in a specific sense, to those dock-labourers who transported cumbrous and heavy loads.

558

one's line of country. *a matter one is interested in and, especially, has knowledge of.* The metaphor is from fox-hunting. Each hunt has its own fields etc. to which it confines its activities. The phrase is generally used negatively: e.g. 'That is not my line of country'.

559

a lion in the path. *an obstacle or danger in one's way.*

560

beard the lion: see 41.

561

put one's head into the lion's mouth: see 502.

562

the lion's share. *the greater profit or benefit that one party in a transaction receives or insists on taking.* The phrase is based on one of Aesop's Fables, though not closely, because in that a lion, having, with the help of other animals, killed a deer, insists with threats on taking for himself not merely the larger part of the animal, but the whole of it.

563

A little bird told me. This is a jocular way of saying one has heard something, without divulging who was the informant. The reference is to a passage in the Bible (*Ecclesiastes*, 10, 20): 'Curse not the king, no not in thy thought; and curse not the rich man in thy bedchamber: for a bird of the air shall carry the voice, and that which hath wings shall tell the matter'.

564

lock, stock, and barrel. *entirely, the whole* (of the thing referred to). The lock, stock, and barrel of a gun make the complete weapon.

565

lock the stable door after the horse is stolen. *take precautions too late, when the mischief is done.* The metaphor appears in many languages. Stevenson cites 1370 as the earliest use in English.

566

the long arm of coincidence. In this metaphor coincidence is personified as a being with a long arm that stretches far so as to bring together widely separated events or circumstances that have no apparent causal connection.

567

in the long run. *in the final result.* The allusion is to horse-racing, where a runner may for a time be leading, but at the end another competitor may win.

568

look a gift-horse in the mouth. *examine a present too critically.* The expression is nearly always used negatively, in an injunction that this is an undesirable thing to do. A horse's age is judged by the condition of its teeth.

569

at a loose end: see 279.

570

What one loses on the swings one gains on the roundabouts. *loss on one article, transaction, etc., is compensated by profit on another.* In a poem by Mr. P. R. Chalmers (1912) there is a line:

> What's lost upon the roundabouts we pull up on the swings.

571

(1) **to lose (or break) the thread; (2) to pick up the threads.** (1) *in conversation; in a speech; or, less commonly, in writing, to diverge from the main line of one's argument, theme, etc.* The allusion seems to be to the thread in the shuttle of a loom, or to the threads that in sewing keep a garment together.

(2) Similarly 'to pick up the threads' (generally plural) refers to circumstances when, after an absence from an occupation for a considerable time, one returns to it and becomes again conversant with and expert at it.

572

to be down on one's luck. *to have one's affairs going, or to have had them go, wrong; to have been unlucky.* For 'on' one would expect 'in'. 'down' = 'brought down low'.

573

mad as a hatter. *quite mad.* Why a man who makes hats should be taken as typical of a madman is unknown. Lewis Carroll popularised the collocation of the words in *Alice in Wonderland*, but it was known earlier: e.g. by Thackeray in *Pendennis*. Brewer conjectures that 'hatter' was a corruption of 'adder', but says that 'evidence is wanting', and *S.O.E.D.* makes no mention of this.

574

mad as a March hare. *quite mad.* Hares in March, which is their breeding season, are especially wild, leaping madly about.

575

make a virtue of necessity. *pretend that what you do under compulsion you do from a sense of duty (as a virtue), or that you like doing it.* The expression goes back to Chaucer.

576

make anything of it. *understand it.* The phrase is generally used only negatively: e.g. 'I can't make anything of it'. 'anything' = 'any sense'. Compare **make head or tail of it (500).**

577

make bricks without straw. *produce something without the necessary material or means.* Straw is to protect bricks from drying, before being burnt in a kiln. The allusion is to a passage in the Bible (*Exodus*, 5), where Pharaoh refuses to provide straw for the Israelites in captivity, and orders that they shall collect their own stubble and yet provide as many bricks as before.

578

make ends (or both ends) meet: see 283.

579

make hay of. *ruin or throw into confusion.* 'These new rules made hay of all our carefully prepared arrangements.' When one makes hay, one cuts down the growing grass, and, after it has dried, turns it over and tosses it about.

580

make hay while the sun shines. *seize the opportunity to do a thing while circumstances are favourable.* 'make hay': do the necessary tossing of the hay, so that it dries; 'while the sun shines': while the weather is dry and warm. Compare **Strike while the iron is hot** (892).

581

make head or tail of it: see 500.

582

make it. (S) This is a phrase of only recent years, meaning *manage to do something that is intended or desired:* e.g. make an appointment, catch a train. 'If you can't make it, come back and spend the night here.'

583

make mincemeat (of). *utterly refute and expose the worthlessness (of).* The phrase is always used with reference to arguments that have been put forward. Their destruction is described in terms that would be used for cutting meat into small fragments.

584

make no bones. *have no hesitation or qualms* about doing or saying something: e.g. pay no attention to considerations one would think might deter a person. The expression is recorded as being used as far back as the middle of the sixteenth century. The allusion may have been to a person who pays no attention to any bones he comes across in soup he is drinking, but swallows everything, 'making': i.e. 'causing to be', and so 'leaving', no bones in the bowl. An alternative conjecture suggested to me is that the allusion is to a person who in cutting up meat shears through the bones.

585

make one's gorge rise. *cause violent or indignant anger or disgust*. The metaphor comes from the action of vomiting. Primarily the 'gorge' was the throat. Then it came to be used for what was swallowed by the throat.

586

make one's hair stand on end: see 284.

587

make rings round a person. *defeat a person thoroughly in a game or other competition*. The allusion is to a victorious boxer able to move round his opponent and rain blows on to him from all directions.

588

the man in the street. *the ordinary man*. The Greville Memoirs (1831) mention the term as used then for a racing man.

589

mealy-mouthed. (a person) *avoiding frank, open, words and statements*, especially from prudery. The idiom seems to be a figurative extension of the image of a person speaking as if he had a soft substance in his mouth, like meal, that prevents vigorous, outright utterance.

All of the following words and phrases refer to a state of mental unsoundness that falls short of what is understood by 'mad' (when used with serious import) and 'insane'. Some that are not marked (S), as slang, are colloquialisms or on the border-line between these and established literary idioms.

590

barmy (or **balmy**). (S) *crazy*. The spelling 'balmy' must have come about by false association with the noun 'balm' and its adjective that means primarily 'yielding an aromatic substance', and so figuratively 'of healing virtue' (connected with 'balsam', from Latin *balsamum*; and compare 'balm of Gilead': see *Genesis*, 37, 25). But 'barm' is the froth that forms on the top of fermenting liquors. There used to be an extended expression, now obsolete: 'barmy on the crumpet', where 'crumpet' was slang for 'head'. Compare 'loaf' and 'crust': see **Use your loaf** (978).

591

batty (or **bats**, which is strictly a noun, but is used adjectivally) are two of the most recent slang words meaning 'crazy'. They are derived from the expression 'bats in the belfry', likening the brain of a person haunted by crazy notions to the belfry of a church infested by bats. Compare the expression **have a bee in one's bonnet** (48); but 'bats' implies a more general and serious state of mental instability than the buzzing through one's head of a single notion in a brain that otherwise may be sound and able.

592

dotty. (S) *feeble-minded, half idiotic.* This may be a figurative extension of the description of a person whose gait, instead of being firmly uniform and even, along straight lines, moves erratically from point to point: is dotted about. There are colloquial phrases 'dotty' and 'dotty on his pins' that refer to a person shaky on his legs. Dr. Sydney Cole suggests that the meaning of the word may be connected with music, because, if in a sequence of even crochets one crochet is dotted, the rhythm becomes irregular.

593

gaga, like **batty** or **bats** (see 591) and **scatty** and **screwy** (601 and 602), is among the more recent slang words that have tended to displace older words and phrases like **barmy, potty, with a screw loose.** The word came to us about 1920 from France, where it was originally used in painting circles. *O.E.D.*, defining its meaning as 'fatuous, exhibiting senile decay, dotty', says it was invented 'in imitation of idiotic laughter'. Between the two World Wars it was much affected by the Bright Young Things for application to people, and to things, especially books, plays, pictures, music, failing to satisfy their standard.

594

half-baked. (S) This term is closely synonymous with **dotty** (see 592) and **not all there** (12). Brewer thinks the original allusion was to meat pies. My friend, Dr. Sydney Cole, suggests it referred to the poor quality of bricks insufficiently baked.

595

have a screw loose. *be in general mentally deficient*, or *have a crazy notion about a particular thing*. The person is regarded as possessing, in his brain, a piece of machinery that is not working perfectly because a screw is loose.

596

have a slate missing (or loose). (S) *be in general mentally deficient.* Presumably a 'slate' was chosen to provide a comparison between the roof of a building from which something was missing and a human being's head and brain.

597

He is not all (or not quite all) there: see 12.

598

midsummer madness. *temporary craziness.* There used to be a widespread belief that on midsummer night people were apt to think and act insanely.

599

off one's head: see 501.

600

potty (S) is closely synonymous with **dotty** (592) and **not all there** (12). But the word has other slang meanings: 'insignificant', 'trivial', 'petty', 'easy'. (OO).

601

scatty (S) is a more recent word for mentally deficient than any of the others in this section: perhaps a vulgarised abbreviation of 'scatter-brained'.

602

screwy. (S) This is another of the more recent synonyms of **dotty,** etc. The word has had a varied history. Its first meaning, going back to 1820, was 'drunk', and there was a participial adjective 'screwed'. About a hundred years ago it came to be used with the sense of 'stingy', 'mean', given to 'screwing'; and there was a noun for a stingy person, 'a screw'. About the same time it had another meaning, applied to a horse, of 'unsound'; again with a noun 'a screw'. It now means 'crazy', perhaps with reference to **a screw lose** (595); but in a still later development it is being used to mean 'fraudulent', with reference to a person or an enterprise etc. Compare the sarcastic expression, 'He is as straight as a corkscrew'.

603

soft. In the sense of 'mentally deficient', 'half-witted', this word goes back over three centuries, and is so used by Burton in *The Anatomy of Melancholy*. *O.E.D.* gives also the meanings 'lacking common sense', 'easily imposed upon or deceived'. There is also the noun 'a softy' (or 'softie'). Compare 'softening of the brain', popular name for progressive dementia with general paresis. (OO)

604

have a tile missing (or **loose**) means the same as 596.

605

mince matters. *express oneself politely in condemnation, or belittle the seriousness, of a situation, so as to soften facts, circumstances, arguments, etc.* The allusion is to making tough meat more tender, palatable, or digestible, by mincing it. The phrase is generally used negatively. For a positive use see *Othello*, II, iii, 243: 'Thy honesty and love doth mince the matter'.

606

mind (or **be on**) **one's P's and Q's.** *be extremely careful in what one says or does.* The reference is usually to conduct in company. The origin of the expression is not certain, though several explanations have been offered and are mentioned by Brewer. One is that it was a warning to school-children, learning to write, that they must exercise care in the formation of these two letters, to make them distinct from one another. Compare **dot one's i's and cross one's t's** (256). Another explanation is that it was a warning to printers' apprentices in setting up type. A third is that in public houses accounts of customers for beer were scored with P's for pints and Q's for quarts. A fourth is that in France, when huge wigs were worn, and bows were made with great formality, teachers of deportment and dancing used to warn their pupils to pay attention to their *pieds* ('feet'), and to their *queues* ('wigs') that might easily be deranged or fall off.

607

miss the bus. *be too late for, or fail to seize, a favourable opportunity to do something.*

608

a month of Sundays. **(S)** *a long tedious period.* As a month has from twenty-eight to thirty-one days, a 'month of Sundays' would mean about thirty Sundays in succession. An alternative explanation is that, as a week is seven days, a 'month of Sundays' might mean seven weeks. Sunday—the Sabbath—used to be in this country, for many people within living memory, a dull day, from which all amusement was debarred, and going to church was the only activity. As we have sensibly said good-bye to all that, the expression will probably soon become obsolete.

609

More power to your elbow! *May your efforts be even more effective and successful!* This is a metaphor taken from manual work that needs powerful drive from the elbow. For 'elbow' see also 276 and 277.

610

Mrs. Grundy. *The conventional dictates of British propriety, especially prudery.* Mrs. Grundy is a character from a play called *Speed the Plough* (1798) by Thomas Morton. She never appears, but is constantly referred to by a Mrs. Ashfield, wondering what Mrs. Grundy will think or say.

611

nail to the counter. *expose so as to be perfectly clear.* The phrase is now always used with reference to a lie. Shopkeepers used to nail counterfeit coins to the counter (presumably as a warning).

612

namby-pamby. The term is applied, as an adjective, (a) to people and actions: *weakly sentimental;* (b) to style in writing: *insipidly pretty.* In sense (a) it is sometimes used as a noun. The term is a fanciful formation of the name of Ambrose Philips (died 1744), author of pastoral poetry ridiculed by Pope in *The Dunciad.*

613

a near miss. *a failure that was nearly a success:* i.e. the opposite of 'a near thing', 'a close thing' (see the next article but one). As often, language is illogical. 'A near miss' ought to mean something that 'nearly misses', but here it means something that 'nearly hits'. (See note at the end of 615.)

614

a near (or **close) shave.** *narrow miss or escape from something undesirable.* A 'shave' is used here in its sense of a slight grazing touch; and a 'close shave' is a narrow escape from touching. (See note at the end of next article.)

615

a near (or close) thing. *a success that was nearly a failure.* For the words to bear the meaning that the phrase has, one must, in an analysis of them, take 'near' and 'close' to be elisions of 'near to failure' and 'close to failure'.

A distinction between the three expressions in 613–15 may be formulated as follows:

a near miss = something that did not happen, but nearly did.

a near shave = 'a near miss', but usually refers to something undesirable.

a near thing = something that did happen, but only just did.

616

break the neck: see 96.

617

get it in the neck. see 423.

618

neck and crop. *entirely*, *altogether*, *thoroughly*, *headlong.* In its primary use a person can be said to be thrown out 'neck and crop'. Figuratively one can be said to drop a thing, or sever relations with a person, 'neck and crop'; rarely, to take up a thing 'neck and crop'. The connection between the words and the meaning is obscure. Why are 'neck and crop' taken as a symbol of entirety? The 'crop' of a bird is the lower part of its neck. A conjecture offered me is that 'crop' may be a corruption of 'croup': the hind-quarters of an animal, especially a horse, and that 'neck and crop' would therefore mean, if not the whole, a large part, of the animal, almost equivalent to 'head to heel', 'tip to toe'.

619

neck and neck. *level, in a race, competition, contest.* The phrase comes from horse-racing where two horses running level have their necks side by side.

620

neck or nothing. This phrase expresses, says *S.O.E.D.*, determination to take all risks, even of being hanged.

621

a nest-egg. (figuratively) *a sum of money kept in reserve for emergency, etc.* This use dates back to the eighteenth century. A literal use dates back a century earlier, meaning an egg, natural or artificial, left in a domestic hen's nest to induce it to go on laying there.

622

nigger in the wood pile. (S) *hidden motive* (especially of an underhand action). The phrase, says Brewer, was originally used with reference to the disappearance of wood and fuel, presumably in U.S.A.

623

cut off one's nose to spite one's face: see 191.

624

keep one's (or another's) nose down to the grindstone: see 532.

625

led by the nose. *easily influenced to do what is suggested by others.* The allusion is to bulls and bears, which are led by a strap or rope coming from a ring through their noses; or to horses and asses, which are led by a strap or rope attached to a bit in the mouth, and encircling the nose. Iago says of Othello that he could be 'led by the nose as asses are' (I, iii, 400).

626

pay through the nose. *pay an exortionate amount.* In spite of two explanations that Brewer offers of this expression, the first recorded use of which is by Andrew Marvell in 1672, it is necessary to mark it (OO).

627

put a person's nose out of joint. (1) *supplant, supersede, a person,* causing him to show discomposure, especially jealousy. The nose has no 'joint', but *C.O.D.* gives 'out of joint', with reference to bone, as meaning 'dislocated'. Perhaps the nose was chosen by the inventor of the metaphor for the part of the body to be injured because it is the most prominent feature of the face, which is the part of the body we chiefly associate with our usual image of a person. The use of the expression is recorded as going back to 1581.

628

Nosey Parker. *inquisitive person habitually trying to pry* (*poke his nose*) *into other people's* (*especially their private*) *affairs.* (OO)

629

not a leg to stand on. *no sound argument or excuse.* A person without sound argument etc. is compared to one who is so unsteady on his legs that he cannot stand up.

630

not a patch on. *not fit to be compared with, not anything as good as.* One of the meanings of 'patch' given by

S.O.E.D. is 'a small scrap, piece, or remnant of anything' (dating back to the sixteenth century). In that sense 'not a patch' means 'not (to be regarded as) even a small scrap', 'on' must stand for 'in relation to', 'in comparison with'. As a meaning of 'on' *S.O.E.D.* gives 'indicating that to which a quality has relation'.

631

not fit to hold a candle to him. *unable* (in effectiveness or some other quality) *to be compared with him.* The phrase is always used negatively. 'He is a good fellow, but in ability and industry cannot hold a candle to his brother.' Its origin is obscure. Brewer says that the reference is to link-boys who held candles in theatres.

632

not let the grass grow under one's feet: see 365.

633

not room to swing a cat: see 248.

634

not to be sneezed (or **sniffed**) **at.** *not to be treated as unimportant.* (The metaphor is used only negatively.) There is a sound from the nose: a slightly audible sneer, not involuntary, however, like a sneeze, nor so loud, that is indicative of contempt.

635

One cannot see the wood for the trees. *One is prevented by a multitude of details from forming a clear general conception.* The early forms of the expression, from John Heywood (1546) to Swift (1738), had 'for trees', without 'the' as in the current form.

636

One cannot make a silk purse out of a sow's ear. *It is impossible to turn a person who is by nature coarse or stupid into a refined and intelligent person.*

James Howell (1594–1666) wrote of the impossibility of making a 'satin purse out of a sow's ear'; John Ray, in *English Proverbs* (1870), of 'making velvet' out of it. 'silk' is recorded first as used by Swift (1738).

637

One cannot put the clock back. *It is impossible to undo changes, social, political, economic, etc., that have happened, so as to make conditions revert to what they were in the past.*

G. K. Chesterton in one of his essays deals with the statement in his often paradoxical and sometimes perverse way, saying it is false: that the clock can be put back because it was made by man, and what man has done he can undo.

638

be nuts on. (S) *be extremely fond of.* There is an even stronger expression: **dead nuts on.** (OO)

639

for nuts. (S) *at all.* The phrase is always used negatively: e.g. 'He can't play golf for nuts'. Perhaps the metaphor comes from a time when nuts were regarded as a great luxury, and the meaning was that a person could not do a certain thing whatever reward were offered to him.

640

O.K. *All correct.* The symbol (or abbreviation, if it is that) has spread widely from U.S.A. into English and into other European and even into Asiatic languages. This has happened in the present century, but the term goes back to the early part of last century. Brewer says it is probably derived from an American Indian (Choctaw) phrase, *oke*, meaning 'It is so'. He adds that Andrew Jackson, the American President (1829–37), used the phrase, and that in the presidential campaign his political opponents said that he had derived it from his own uneducated spelling: 'Orl Korect'. The expression no doubt owes its popularity to the convenience of its shortness and ease in pronunciation and writing compared with words and phrases it has to a great extent displaced: e.g. 'Right', 'All right', 'That's all right', 'Very well'; and to an onomatopoeic quality suggestive of vigorous affirmation. It is now used also as an adjective ('That is quite O.K.') and a verb ('I had to get the secretary to O.K. the scheme').

641

odour of sanctity. *reputation for holiness.* The expression is generally used with reference to a person's dying. Originally the phrase meant the sweet smell that was supposed to be exhaled from the bodies of dying or exhumed saints.

642

out-Herod Herod. *exceed in wickedness even the most notoriously wicked character.* King Herod is taken as a prime example of wickedness on account of the crimes he committed, especially his ordering the massacre of the children in Bethlehem.

'I would have such a fellow whipped for o'er doing Termagant; it out-Herods Herod' (*Hamlet*, III, ii). Termagant and Herod were favourite characters in the old miracle plays. The first was an imaginary god of the Saracens; the second was represented as the typical tyrant.

643

paddle one's own canoe. *manage one's affairs without help or interference.*

644

be at pains; take pains. *be at, take, trouble.* 'I was at considerable pains to explain my attitude.' 'He took great pains to make the affair a success.' 'pain', which now ordinarily means 'suffering', used to have the meaning of 'trouble'.

645

for one's pains. *in return for one's exertions or trouble.* 'All he got for his pains was a curt acknowledgement.'

646

on (or **under**) **pain.** *with the punishment, penalty, to be incurred.* 'That can be done only under pain of death.' The idiom is now obsolescent.

647

pains and penalties. *punishments.* 'The Act then sets out the pains and penalties. This pleonastic phrase belongs to the class of 'idiomatic idiosyncrasies' as Pearsall Smith calls phrasal collocations in which two words are habitually used together for the sake of emphasis.

648

paint the lily. *unnecessarily and absurdly try to embellish what is already perfectly beautiful.* The phrase comes from *King John*, IV, ii, 11:

> To gild refined gold, to paint the lily,
> To throw a perfume on the violet,

To smooth the ice, or add another hue
Unto the rainbow, or with taper-light
To seek the beauteous eye of heaven to garnish,
Is wasteful and ridiculous excess.

The phrase is sometimes misquoted as 'gild the lily'.

649

beyond the pale. *outside the limits of decent society.* 'pale' originally referred to the district in Ireland where from the twelfth century English Law prevailed. A meaning of the Middle English noun 'pale' was a 'paling'.

650

palm off. *impose (on a person) by trickery or fraud (a thing of little or no value).* This use of the verb 'palm' is connected with the action of a conjurer or cheater at cards who conceals things in the palm of his hands.

651

palmy days: see 210.

652

a Parthian shot (or shaft). *a wounding remark at parting.* The ancient Parthians, of Western Asia, were said to be adepts at shooting arrows backward at their enemies, as they rode away in full flight.

653

pass the time of day: see 211.

654

patience on a monument. *great patience.* The quality of patience is here pictured as a statue on a pedestal typical of immovable endurance. 'She sat like Patience on a monument, smiling at grief' (*Twelfth Night*, II, iv, 114).

655

a Paul Pry. *one who habitually is inquisitive about and meddles in his neighbours' private affairs.* The allusion is to the chief character in a comedy called *Paul Pry* (1825) by John Poole.

656

pay (or **pay back**) **in his own coin.** *retaliate by using on an opponent the same methods he employed against one.* The expression (of which the first recorded use is by Robert Greene in 1589) is equivalent to **give tit for tat** (see 953).

657

pay on the nail. *pay at once,* directly a transaction is made, contrasted with being allowed credit. At one time the expression was thought to be connected with pillars, called Nails, at Exchanges at Liverpool and elsewhere, with metal plates, on which bargains were settled. Brewer points out, however, that this cannot be the origin of the phrase, because it was common in the sixteenth century, long before Exchanges existed, and Pearsall Smith includes it in a list of idioms 'for which even specialists have not been able to find a completely certain explanation'. Mr. Eric Partridge has since suggested that it came from flipping a coin, with one's nail, to a pot-boy.

658

pay a person out. *punish a person, in retaliation for an injury,* by an action that, to use another metaphor, will 'serve him right'.

659

pay the piper. *pay whatever the cost is* (literally or figuratively). The allusion is to the person who at a party pays the piper to lead the dance. There is also a saying 'He who pays the piper should (or may) call the tune' = 'He who pays the cost has (or should have) the right to decide what is to be done'.

660

pay through the nose: see 626.

661

the devil to pay: see 234.

662

peter out. *come to an end. O.E.D.* says this was originally a mining colloquialism from U.S.

663

to pick up the threads: see 571.

664

at a pinch. *at* (*or in*) *an extremity.* The phrase goes back to the fifteenth century. J. S. Whitehead in *Everyday English Phrases* (1937) says 'He will get through at a pinch' means 'He will only just succeed at the cost of being pinched': i.e. 'squeezed', 'pressed'.

665

in the pink. (*S.O.E.D.* classes the expression as 'colloquial or slang'.) *in perfect health.* 'pink' is in this phrase used absolutely, but there are phrases such as 'in the pink of health', 'the pink of perfection'. 'pink' (derivation unknown) was primarily a noun and the name of various species of the flower *dianthus*. Then it came to be used for the perfection of some good quality: the 'flower' of excellence; and only later was it used as an adjective, of colour.

666

the pipe of peace. The origin of the phrase was the habit among the American Indians, when they met on friendly terms to settle differences, of celebrating the occasion by smoking a pipe. The pipe (calumet) was a reed about two feet long, with a bowl of clay decorated with feathers. Today 'to smoke the pipe of peace' would mean to renew relations with a person with whom one had quarrelled, by meeting him in a friendly way over a drink and smoke.

667

the piping times of peace. *the happy old days when there were no wars or rumours of wars.* The metaphor is that of people amusing themselves with pastoral pipes instead of martial drums and fifes. It dates back to at all events the sixteenth century, and appears in Gloucester's opening speech in *Richard III:* 'in this weak piping time of peace' (I, i, 24).

668

as plain as a pikestaff. *clear and unmistakable.* A 'pikestaff' was a staff on which a pedlar supported his bundle when standing to rest. 'pikestaff' is an alteration of an earlier phrase, which was 'as plain as a packstaff'. 'plain', says the *Oxford Book of Proverbs*, was a reference to its plain (i.e. undecorated) surface.

669

have too much on one's plate. *have too many jobs to do.* The image is of a person who has more food on his plate than he can eat. Compare **have too many irons in the fire** (525).

670

play ducks and drakes. *squander one's money.* In its primary use the expression means to throw stones into water so that they skim over the surface with a bouncing motion. In its figurative use a person squandering money is regarded as throwing it about recklessly for mere amusement. (Compare the colloquial expression for extravagant and showy expenditure, 'make a splash'.) Its use goes back to Florio, Chapman, Shirley, in the early and middle seventeenth century.

671

play second fiddle. *take a subordinate position*, whether in an official or private capacity.

672

play the devil (or deuce) with: see 233.

673

play to the gallery. *aim at impressing the vulgar crowd.* The allusion is to an actor who aims at winning popularity among the less educated members of his audience in the gallery, instead of the more educated in the higher priced seats of the theatre.

674

to play up to. (1) *The chief primary meaning of the expression is employed with reference to the part played by a person on the stage in connection with assisting another actor.* (2) *to flatter or to toady.* (3) *to back up.*

675

play. For idioms, based on games, into which the word 'play' enters, see 381, 382, 383, 397, 398, 406, 411.

676

plough the sands. *engage in a task that can have no results, or is endless.* The first recorded use of the metaphor is by Greene in 1588.

677

a pot (usually **a big pot**). *a person of importance.* It is not clear how a 'pot', rather than some other domestic article: e.g. a plate, cup, glass, jug, came to be selected, for purposes of metaphors, as the object that, if it were large, could be a symbol of importance. But there are analogous uses of 'pot'. *S.O.E.D.* gives it as (colloquially) meaning a large sum of money; (slang) a large sum betted or staked; (in racing) a horse backed for a large amount, or a favourite.

In distinction with these meanings of 'pot' compare 'potty' in its sense of 'insignificant' etc.: see 600.

Synonymous slang terms for **a big pot** are **a big bug** (see 55) and **a big wig.**

678

go to pot: see 450.

679

keep the pot boiling: see 533.

680

take pot luck. *be willing to eat whatever food there happens to be for a meal, not specially prepared for a guest.* Literally the phrase means to take what is in the pot on the fire, containing a stew or what not. The phrase may have originated when each of the people eating a meal ladled out mouthfuls for himself from a common stock-pot.

681

the pot calling the kettle black. *a person charging another with a fault he himself commits.* The *Oxford Book of English Proverbs* does not cite a record of this expression; but it gives a delightful quotation from the first translation into English of *Don Quixote*, by Thomas Shelton, in 1620: 'Methinks, sir . . . you are like what is said that the frying pan said to the kettle, "Avaunt, blackbrows"; you reprehend me for speaking of proverbs, and you thread up yours by two and two together'.

682

a pound of flesh. *full payment, however harsh the terms may be.* The allusion is to the bargain made by Shylock with Antonio in *The Merchant of Venice.*

683

pour oil on troubled waters. *bring about appeasement in a disturbed condition.* The allusion is to the flattening effect of oil on waves.

684

the powers that be. *the constituted authorities*, or sometimes more loosely *the influential people controlling matters.* 'be', instead of 'are', is an archaic form. The phrase comes in the Bible (*Romans*, 13, 1).

685

a pretty pickle. *a difficulty, a troublesome state of affairs, a disagreeable situation, a sorry plight.* 'pickle' here is a metaphor from the acidity of the mixture of salt, vinegar, etc.

in which pickles are made. 'pretty', or some other epithet, is used ironically. Compare **a pretty kettle of fish** (348), and phrases like 'a nice mess', 'a fine muddle'.

686

only pretty Fanny's way. *only a customary way a person (man or woman) has of acting or speaking that one need not take seriously.* The phrase, which comes from a poem by Thomas Parnell (1697–1717), is not as popular today as it used to be some years ago. It is used in an ironic or contemptuous spirit for pretending, in discredit of something a person has done or said, to dismiss it as merely a harmless trait.

687

prick up one's ears. *have one's attention suddenly roused.* This is a metaphor from a dog, or a horse, which erects its ears when on the alert. 'prick up' is not used in any other context.

688

the primrose path. *the path of pleasure.* As this expression comes in *Hamlet* (I, iii, 50) and in *Macbeth* (II, iii), it may have been a common Elizabethan phrase.

689

The proof of the pudding is in the eating: see 275.

690

the psychological moment. *the suitable, critical, moment, to do something, or at which something happens.* The phrase seems to have originated in a German one, in which 'moment' stood, not for a unit of time, but for 'momentum'. The English phrase, with the philosophical associations of the adjective, has been taken up eagerly by journalists anxious to impress their readers. Its application is often absurdly inept. Thus in the gardening notes of a newspaper we are told that 'the present showery weather provides a psychological moment for transplanting lettuce seedlings'.

691

pull a person's leg. *say something that* (1) *befools, deceives, or is intended to deceive, a person;* or (2) *is not intended to be taken seriously: a sort of joke.* (OO)

692

pull one's weight. *do one's share in contributing to a result.* The image is that of a person who in e.g. walking pulls along by his own effort the weight of his body, and does not remain passive while somebody does this for him, as for example if he were in a boat in which another did the rowing. Perhaps the allusion is to boat-racing. I have heard the phrase applied negatively to a person who was described as in company merely listening without doing his share of contributing to the conversation.

693

(1) **pull strings;** (2) **pull the strings.** (1) *be able to exert personal and private influence* (on a matter affecting oneself or others). (2) *be the person who controls affairs,* even if nominally somebody else is above him. The metaphors are from puppetry.

694

pull the chestnuts out of the fire: see a cat's-paw (245).

695

put a false colour on: see 160.

696

get (or **put**) **a person's back up:** see 246.

697

put a person's nose out of joint: see 627.

698

put a spoke in a person's wheel. *thwart a person's plans or arrangements.* The phrase is based on the use of the word 'spoke' in the sense of a bar used to prevent the wheel of a vehicle from turning, especially when going down hill.

699

put all one's eggs in one basket: see 18.

700

put on the slate (against a person). This means the same as, and has a similar origin to, **chalk up** (against a person): see 135.

701

put on side. (S) *assume a swaggering, superior attitude; give oneself airs.* Pearsall Smith says that the metaphor may have come from billiards. There 'side' means the direction given to a ball by striking it at a point not directly in the middle. He does not offer an explanation of the connection between this and the figurative meaning.

702

put on the screw. (S) *force a person to do something.* The image is of a screw that works a press.

703

put one's foot down: see 366.

704

put one's foot in it: see 367.

705

put one's hand to the plough: see 474.

706

put one's head in the lion's mouth: see 502.

707

put (or **lay** or **set**) **one's shoulder to the wheel.** *set to work vigorously. S.O.E.D.* says that literally the reference is to extricating a vehicle from the mud. One of Aesop's fables tells of a carter who, when the wheel of his wagon became fixed in a rut, called for help from Hercules. Hercules arrived on the scene, but rebuked the man for not first having put his shoulder to the wheel, and tried to extricate it by his own efforts, before calling on the gods for help.

708

Put that in your pipe and smoke it. This is a rather rude way of saying to a person: '*Now that you know what I have told you, there is something for you to think about that I hope will make you feel uncomfortable*'.

709

put the cart before the horse. *reverse the natural or proper order; take what is the effect for the cause.* The first recorded approach to the image goes back as far as 1340, in a prose work called *Remorse of Conscience*: 'Many religious teachers set the plough before the oxen'. In 1520 Robert Whitinton in *Vulgaria* has 'That teacher setteth the carte before the horse that preferreth imitacyon before preceptes'. In 1589 Puttenham's *Arte of English Poesie* refers to 'the cart before the horse' as 'a proverb'.

710

put the lid on it. (S) *be the culminating event that ends or settles the matter.* Literally, when a lid is put on a box, jar, etc., this completes some process. Figuratively the phrase is always used with reference to an undesired, unwelcome, event.

711

put two and two together. *find out something, reach a conclusion, when a connection between things that have been done or said is borne in on our consciousness.* But why 'two and two' (four things altogether) instead of 'one and one' (two things altogether)?

712

stay put. *remain where one is, refuse to move.* The phrase is used both literally with reference to physical position, and figuratively with reference to conduct, for not budging from an attitude or course one has taken. By many people it would be regarded today as slang or colloquial, and it has not yet reached *C.O.D.*, but it will probably become established in literary English. As Mr. M. R. Ridley has said, it has a 'fine, solid, stone-walling, in some contexts even a hint of backs-to-the-wall, immobility about it which no equivalent quite gives'.

713

a Pyrrhic victory. *a victory gained at such cost that it is almost equivalent to a defeat.* The reference is to the defeat of the Romans by Pyrrhus, King of Epirus, at Asculum, 280 B.C. To those who came to congratulate him he said: 'Another such victory and we are done for'.

714

queer a person's pitch. *spoil a person's undertakings.* The expression in its literal sense refers to a person who does something to spoil the trade of a street or market seller.

715

in Queer Street. *in difficulties* (perhaps especially financial). *S.O.E.D.*'s definition is 'an imaginary street in which people in difficulties reside'. In the legal quarter of London there is a Carey Street where the Bankruptcy Buildings are situated, and 'to be in Carey Street' is an expression often applied in a general way to people and firms in financial difficulties. Perhaps there is a connection between this use of Carey Street and Queer Street.

716

on the Q T (or **q t**). *secretly;* often with a bad sense, *surreptitiously.* Obviously it is an abbreviation of 'quiet'.

717

rack and ruin. The words are used with the verb 'go to'. 'rack' here is perhaps a variant of 'wrack' = 'wreckage' = 'wreck'. The phrase is generally applied to buildings, but it could refer to e.g. a business.

718

for a rainy day: see 208.

719

It never (or **seldom**) **rains but it pours.** *Events of bad and good fortune do not come singly.* The statement is generally applied to misfortunes. The earliest records of the saying in English are cited in 1726, when it was used by Pope, Swift, and Arbuthnot.

720

raise Cain. *make a violent disturbance:* raise the spirit, as it were, of Cain, who, as the murderer of his brother, is taken as a symbol of unrestrained violence.

721

raise the wind. *arrange to get money, especially by borrowing.* (For the use of the verb compare 'raise a loan'.) The origin of the metaphor is unknown. If one is to conjecture, the first thought is that, as Pearsall Smith points out many idioms are, it is nautical. In a sailing ship, unless there is wind, a ship is becalmed and is unable to continue on its course. If a man has no money he cannot go ahead with his projects. By borrowing money he 'raises a wind' that extricates him from this state. See 1015 for an old superstition that one might raise a wind by whistling.

722

a raw deal. *unfair, harsh, treatment over a transaction.* This is the only idiom in which 'raw' has that sense.

723

read between the lines. *discern a hidden significance that is not outwardly obvious in something said, written, imagined.*

724

red herring (with reference to 'drawing a red herring across the path'). *side issue to divert attention from the main question.* I am told that in the sport of stag-hunting as a strong-smelling lure for the hounds, aniseed was at one time used, and later a red herring; and it has been conjectured that this deception of the hounds, by the substitution of one thing for another, led to the use of the term in its figurative sense.

725

like a red rag to a bull. *causing a person to be excitedly and violently angry.* I am told by a scientific friend that it is now established that bulls are colour-blind: so toreadors might just as well use cloaks of any other colour than red.

726

red tape. *excessive insistence on formal details, especially in public business.* The origin of the idiom is the use of red tape for tying up documents. This use goes back three centuries or more. Eliezer Edwards cites an advertisement in the *Public Intelligence* of 6th December 1658 offering a reward for the restoration of 'a little bundle of papers tied with red tape lost on Friday last between Worcester House and Lincoln's Inn'.

727

to see red. *be excitedly and violently angry* (1) with a person whom one wishes to kill; (2) about some policy, opinion, etc. The metaphor is based on the idea that the vision of a person in this state is blood-coloured.

728

rest on one's laurels; rest on one's oars. Both these metaphors refer to a person who remains, temporarily or permanently, satisfied with success he has gained, without striving for more. The first metaphor is an allusion to the ancient Greeks, who gave the victor in the Pythian Games a wreath of laurels; the second to an oarsman who, after finishing a strenuous course, stops rowing and lets his hand remain on the oar ('rest on' = 'remain at rest with').

729

ride the high horse. *behave in a superior, haughty, overbearing way; put on airs.* The image is that of a person mounted on a horse so high that he looks down on others riding less high horses or walking. The recorded use of the metaphor does not go back further than early in the last century.

730

ride for a fall. *act in such a dangerous, especially reckless, way, that one will probably come to disaster.* 'for' = 'in such a way as to cause'.

731

ride hell for leather. *ride with furious speed.* The phrase is used only literally with reference to riding on horseback. The syntactical construction of the phrase, and its word for word meaning, are obscure. Does 'leather' refer to the reins, which the rider makes no use of? Or does it refer to the saddle, which on a long ride may become painfully uncomfortable? Does 'hell for' stand for 'to hell with', meaning one does not care what happens to the reins or saddle?

732

ride roughshod over. *treat without any consideration of hurting (a person's) feelings.* The word 'roughshod' in its literal sense refers to horses that are provided with shoes having the nail-heads projecting to prevent slipping. Such shoes would disturb and roughen the surface of the ground over which the horse travelled.

733

ring a bell. *cause one to remember something; rouse a mental echo.* The metaphor is based on the idea that, as the ringing of a bell summons a person to answer it, something said to a person evokes in him an associated thought.

734

rob Peter to pay Paul. *take away from one person, cause, etc., in order to pay or contribute to another,* sometimes with the implication of committing an injustice. *O.E.D.* gives the allocation of the two names as going back to Middle English. (There was sometimes a variant for 'pay', of 'give to' or 'clothe'. John Wycliffe (1380): 'Lord, how should God approve that you rob Peter, and give this robbery to Paul in the name of Christ?') I am indebted to the Rev. W. M. Atkins, Librarian of St. Paul's Cathedral, for the following information that bears on a particular application of the expression in the sixteenth century.

When in 1550 the diocese of Westminster, of which the patron saint is St. Peter, and in which is situated Westminster Abbey, was rejoined to that of London, the manors of Paddington and Westbourne, formerly the possession of Westminster Abbey, were transferred to the diocese of London, in which is situated St. Paul's Cathedral, of which the patron saint is St. Paul. This transaction probably contributed to the popularity of the expression **rob Peter to pay Paul.**

735

a Roland for an Oliver. *a blow for a blow; an effective retort; tit for tat; to give as good as you get.* Roland and Oliver were two Knights of Charlemagne celebrated for their exploits. What Oliver did Roland did; and vice versa. At last they fought in single combat for five days, but neither could gain an advantage over the other.

736

a rolling stone. *a person who never remains long in one situation, occupation, etc.* There is a proverb 'A rolling stone gathers no moss', which is capable of two interpretations, according to the context: that such a person does not become encrusted with dull, set, fixed habits or opinions; or that he does not attain a position of security, prosperity, success. The proverb is recorded as far back as the middle of the fifteenth century.

737

rope in. *induce to co-operate* (in a job, scheme, organization, etc.).

738

a rough diamond. *a person without much education, culture, social manners, but not lacking virtues of character etc.* A diamond before it has been cut is a dull, unshowy stone.

739

a round robin. *a petition with signatures in a circle,* so that the order in which they were written is not disclosed. This arrangement was originally used by sailors. Why the word 'robin' was used is unknown.

740

round-table conference. *political or other conference attended by representatives of various interests to discuss matters and reach agreement.* Today the table at which the representatives sit may not be round, but the idea originally was that a round table prevented there being a head-seat, and that all present should be on equal terms, without any jealousy on the score of precedence.

An article by Brewer has some interesting information about round tables. Details of the legendary Round Table of King Arthur come from Malory's *Morte d'Arthur*, but such tables, he points out, were common in the age of chivalry. He refers to the one shown at Winchester, used to accommodate twelve favourite knights of Henry III, which Henry VIII showed to Francis I; to a table established at Kenilworth in the reign of Edward I by Roger Mortimer; and one erected by Edward III at Windsor.

741

rub in. *emphasise or reiterate* (especially something disagreeable). The image is perhaps that of a person who, in applying ointment to relieve pain, rubs so vigorously that the pain is aggravated.

742

by rule of thumb. *in a rough and ready way:* i.e. by rules based on practical experience, as contrasted with theory. The allusion is to using one's thumb as a measure of length.

743

rule the roost. *have full power and authority over others.* The metaphor is commonly supposed to be from a cock that in a henhouse decides where it will perch and what hen or hens shall be nearest to it. *O.E.D.*, however, states that, though the expression was in common use as far back as the sixteenth century, none of the early examples shows any light on its precise origin.

Brewer doubts whether the phrase was originally **rule the roost,** and gives reasons for thinking it was **rule the roast,** and applied to the person who directed the cooking of meat in a kitchen.

744

a run for one's money. *some interest or pleasure or satisfaction though the result may not be a complete success.* The phrase came originally from horse-racing, where a bet on a horse may afford some pleasurable excitement, even if the horse loses.

745

cut and run: see 188.

746

in the long run: see 567.

747

run amuck (or **amok**). *act excitedly, wildly.* **amuck** is a corruption of the Malay word **amok** meaning rushing about in a frenzied thirst for blood. The phrase is recorded in use as far back as 1672, by Andrew Marvell.

748

run one's head against a stone wall: see 503.

749

run riot. *behave in an undisciplined, wild, disorderly way.* The phrase was originally used of hounds that had lost the scent.

750

run the gauntlet. *be subjected to criticism from a number of quarters.* Literally it meant to pass between rows of men who struck one, as military or naval punishment. It is now obsolete in this sense, though still used, for similar practice, by schoolboys. 'gauntlet' here is a corruption, through the French *gantlope*, of the Swedish *gatlopp* (street), which is not connected with 'gauntlet' meaning 'glove' (see 939).

751

run to earth. *after a long search to find a person or thing; get to the bottom of a matter; trace something: e.g. a story, rumour, quotation, to its source.* One metaphorically hunts it ('run' being used in a transitive construction), as a huntsman pursues a fox to the spot where it tries to escape from the hounds by running into its hole in the ground. See **in at the death** (224).

752

The sands are running out. *There is not much more time* (before something will happen or something can be done). The reference is to the sand running through an hour-glass.

753

S O S. *message of extreme urgency appealing for help.* The phrase is sometimes used as, not a noun, but an adjective: e.g. in a broadcast, 'Here is an S O S message for John Smith' (followed by some particulars for identification). It is primarily a code signal used by wireless operators, especially on board ship. Then it came to mean, in general, an appeal for help. The letters are sometimes erroneously thought to stand for 'Save our souls' or 'Save our ship'. Brewer points out that they were adopted for convenience, being three dots, three dashes, three dots.

754

in sackcloth and ashes. This is today a rather exaggerated expression to denote that a person is *penitent for something he admits he ought not to have done.* In the Bible the wearing of sackcloth and ashes is an indication of mourning and sorrow.

755

sail close to the wind. *do something that is perilously near being positively wrong (especially criminally so):* what is sometimes called 'sharp practice'. Sir Alan Herbert in *What a Word!* points out that the current popular meaning of the phrase is not correctly connected with sailing.

The whole art of tacking, he explains, is to sail close to the wind. If one sails too close, the vessel will go slower, or even stop, but this, though showing inefficiency and carelessness, does not show cunning, unscrupulousness, or dishonesty.

756

the salt of the earth. *the most valuable members of the community:* i.e. according to the values of the person using this expression. The expression comes from the Bible, in the Sermon on the Mount, after the beatitudes: 'Ye are the salt of the earth' (*Matthew*, 5, 13).

757

in the same boat. *in a situation in which people share the same fortunes, especially difficulties and dangers.* The people concerned are thought of as passengers in a boat on the sea exposed to wind, waves, etc.

758

in the same box. The general meaning is the same as that of **in the same boat** (last article). Here the metaphor seems to be that of articles packed in the same box.

759

by the same token. *in corroboration of this; the proof of this being that.* The phrase is connected with the use of the word 'token' (dating from Old English) to mean something serving as proof of a fact or statement; evidence. It is generally used today, however, to mean merely 'moreover', and is entered by *S.O.E.D.* as archaic or jocular.

760

tarred with the same brush. *characterised by the same bad qualities.* Brewer says that the reference is to sheep belonging to a flock whose owner has them marked by a brush dipped in tar.

761

The sands are running out: see 752.

762

Satan rebuking sin. *a person rebuking another for a fault of which he himself also is guilty.* Compare **the pot calling the kettle black** (681).

763

save the mark. This phrase, in its current meaning, cannot be transliterated. It is used today merely as an exclamation of ironical apology for something that has just been stated. *S.O.E.D.* says that probably the expression was an exclamatory formula to avert an evil omen, as in the words 'God save (or 'bless') the mark' (compare, for this use of 'save', 'God save the King'); and was then used by way of apology for mentioning anything horrible, disgusting, or profane. There is no evidence, says Brewer, in favour of the belief that the expression arose from archery.

764

goes without saying: see 454.

765

Least said, soonest mended: see 551.

766

He cannot say (or **cry**) **Bo to a goose.** *He is so timid that he can never utter a word to assert himself on any point however small and against anybody however unformidable.* *S.O.E.D.* (which gives also the spelling 'Boh') describes the word as an exclamation intended to surprise or frighten, and compares it with a Latin verb *boare* (= 'to cry aloud', 'to bellow') and a Greek verb *boaein* (= 'to low'), both of which words are from the same root as the Latin *bos* (= a 'cow': genitive *bovis*), and our adjective 'bovine'.

There is also, with the same derivation, the word 'boo' (or 'boh'), as noun signifying contempt or aversion, and as verb meaning to 'hoot' (originally to 'low', of a cow).

In a letter to *The Times*, for leave to quote which acknowledgment is due to the author and *The Times*, the Rev. Bertram Lamplugh writes as follows: 'When I was living in Central Germany over fifty years ago, one frequently came across quite small children driving flocks of geese to pasture and urging the laggards forward with cries of "Boh! Boh!" Probably in earlier days, when more geese were pastured on English greens and commons than nowadays, a similar procedure prevailed, and anyone who could not say "Bo to a goose" would be regarded scornfully and proverbially as more timid than the little gooseherds of the village greens.' The *Oxford Book of English Proverbs* cites also 'He cannot say Bo! to a battledore' (1621), with reference to the clergy of that time; and 'He dare not say Bo! to your blanket' (1721): meaning 'He dare not threaten to inflict the least injury on anyone'.

767

Says you: see 789.

768

what he says goes. *What he says is commonly regarded as authoritative:* if a statement of fact, to be accepted as true; if an order or instruction, to be carried out.

769

when all is said and done: see 19.

770

The scales fell from his eyes: see 296.

771

in a scrape. *in a predicament, in trouble, resulting from imprudence. S.O.E.D.* cites the use of the phrase in this sense as far back as early in the eighteenth century. There is no obvious connection between 'scrape' in its ordinary senses and the meaning in the phrase.

772

scot free. rarely: *without having to pay anything;* usually: *without loss, punishment, penalty.* 'scot' here is an old legal word meaning 'tax'.

773

scotch the snake. *destroy the cause of the evil.* That is the sense in which it is used today. In its primary sense to 'scotch' meant to 'cut', 'gash'. An emendation by Theobald, of a passage in *Macbeth* (III, 1, 13), where Macbeth, speaking of his fears about Banquo, was in the text represented as saying 'We have scorch'd the snake, not killed it', gave the reading 'scotch'd'. Early in the nineteenth century 'scotch' came to be used as a synonym of 'erase', 'stamp out', 'permanently destroy': i.e. with a meaning exactly opposite to Macbeth's ('not killed it'). If one tried today to use it in its original sense, one would be misunderstood. A friend who, as elsewhere, prefers not to be mentioned by name, offers the following conjecture. He points out that, besides the verb to 'scotch', meaning to 'cut', based on Theobald's emendation in *Macbeth*, there is another verb to 'scotch', given independently by *S.O.E.D.*, meaning to block a wheel etc. to prevent it from moving. (Compare 'spoke' in **to put a spoke in a person's wheel: 698.**) A use in this sense is cited in 1642; and there is a noun 'scotch', meaning a block placed under a wheel etc. for the same purpose, whose use is cited as going back to 1601. My friend suggests that Shakespeare used the word in this sense: i.e. Macbeth fears lest even the murder of Banquo he has planned may have only partly and temporarily removed the danger in the witches' prophecy that Banquo's, and not his own, children shall be kings.

774

between Scylla and Charybdis. *between two dangers equally serious:* if a person has to escape from one he runs into the other. Scylla was a legendary monster that lived on an Italian rock; Charybdis was another monster, on the Sicilian side of the strait, that caused a whirlpool. Sailors trying to avoid one of these would often come to disaster from the other. The promontory in the toe of Italy is named Caenys; on the Sicilian side, Pelorum.

775

One cannot see the wood for the trees: see 635.

776

See how the cat jumps: see 251.

777

See how the land lies. *find out the state of affairs,* especially before deciding what course to take. The friend (see 773) to whom I am indebted for many interesting and ingenious suggestions that have been adopted, but who prefers to be anonymous, suggests that the allusion here may be to an artilleryman's examination of the terrain in order to obtain a field of fire; and that this will depend on how the land 'lies': i.e. flat, uphill, down hill.

Compare the next article: **see how the wind blows.**

778

See how the wind blows. *find what the state of affairs is;* especially whether favourable or unfavourable with reference to a project: as, in sailing, one estimates how the direction and strength of the wind will affect one's progress. John Heywood in his collection of proverbs (1546) gives, instead of 'see', 'know which way'.

779

to see red: see 727.

780

seen better days: see 212.

781

sell the pass. *betray a cause.* The origin of the idiom is military, and refers to a narrow passage through mountains viewed as a means to entering and attacking a country.

782

send to Coventry. *ostracise, taboo, boycott, exclude from society.* The origin of this expression may be connected with a passage in Clarendon's *History of the Rebellion* (VI, 837): 'At Birmingham a town so generally wicked that it had risen upon small parties of the king's and killed or taken them prisoners and sent them to Coventry'. (Coventry was then strongly held for the Parliament.) Brewer refers to this explanation in quoting from a *History of Birmingham* by W. Hutton (1723–1815). He mentions another explanation, that at some period (he does not say when) the citizens of Coventry so strongly disliked soldiers that a woman seen speaking to one was regarded as having disgraced herself, and was tabooed; and consequently, when a soldier was stationed at Coventry, he was cut off from social intercourse.

I am indebted to Mr. E. Simpson, City Librarian of Coventry, for a further explanation, based on a note published in the *Coventry Standard* in 1925. The writer of this note considers that the name Coventry is derived from 'covin-tree', which was an oak-tree, standing in front of a castle, on which feudal barons used to hang enemies (see e.g. Scott's *Quentin Durward,* ch. 3). 'Send him to the covin-tree' would be the command, suggests the writer of the note, who adds that the history of Coventry records many notorious people who were sent there for punishment, and considers that it was probably in this connection that the phrase 'send to Coventry' had its origin.

783

separate the sheep from the goats. *divide* (practically, with reference to some purpose for which they are needed; or in one's estimation of them by a moral or intellectual or other standard) *good or useful people from bad or useless.* The wording comes from the Bible (*Matthew*, 25, 32): 'as a shepherd divideth his sheep from the goats': i.e. when wild goats have mingled in the flock.

784

set a stone rolling. *do something that leads to a course of events.* The expression is often used with reference to unforeseen, especially disastrous, results.

785

set by the ears. *cause (people) to quarrel.* I am indebted to Dr. Sydney Cole for the following explanation of the origin. 'This is from dog-fights on which two people have a bet. Each crouches behind his dog, holding its ears so as to make it face the other dog.'

786

set on foot: see 368.

787

set one's teeth on edge. (literally) *cause an unpleasant tingling sensation in the teeth;* (figuratively) *cause distaste or repulsion.* The metaphor comes from the Bible (*Ezekiel*,

18, 2; *Jeremiah*, 31, 29) where the sins of parents who have eaten sour grapes are said to cause their children to suffer ill effects.

A medical friend, while offering no physiological explanation of the unpleasant sensation mentioned, says it is not dependent on teeth, as it can be experienced by those who have lost all their teeth.

788

set the Thames on fire. *do something remarkable; make a brilliant reputation.* The phrase is nearly always used negatively, with reference to a person who is not thought likely to do this. (OO)

789

Sez (or Says) you. (S) *Nonsense.* 'Sez you' is the more common form. This derisive exclamation of contemptuous incredulity, Mr. Eric Partridge says in his *Dictionary of Slang*, came from U.S.A. about 1930.

790

shake the dust from one's feet: see 369.

791

no great shakes. (S) *of no great merit or importance.* The phrase is generally used with a contemptuously derogatory reference to a person. Perhaps, like so many of our idioms, as Pearsall Smith points out, the origin was nautical. For one meaning of the noun 'shake' *S.O.E.D.* gives 'fluttering (of a sail)', and, of the verb *to shake*, 'cause (a sail) to flutter (in the wind)'. Dr. Sydney Cole, however, suggests that the origin of the phrase may be connected with the use of 'shake' (now archaic in this country, though still used in U.S.A.) in the sense of 'quake', as in the word 'earthquake', and so meaning a person who, figuratively, will not cause earthquakes.

792

Shanks's mare. *one's own legs as a means of conveyance.* 'shank' is the leg from knee to ankle. To go somewhere 'on Shanks's mare' is to walk there, sometimes with the implication that there is no opportunity, or one cannot afford, to drive there, go by train, etc. The phrase has now become established as **Shanks's** (or **Shank's**) **mare**, but in the past both 'nag' and 'pony' were used. In the development of proverbs and proverbial sayings the eventual crystallisation often shows a variation from early verbal forms. The Scottish poet Robert Fergusson (1750–74) wrote:

> And auld shanks-naig wad tire, I dread,
> To pace to Berwick.

The *Oxford Book of English Proverbs* records for the earliest use of 'mare' Samuel Bishop, in 1795.

793

sheet-anchor. *one's principal steadying support; the resource on which one relies in difficulties.* In the days of sailing ships the sheet-anchor was a spare anchor for use when the main anchors were not holding a ship, and she was dragging. The cable was not attached to this anchor until needed. Admiral Sir William James, to whom I am indebted for the matter in this note, tells me that in his day it was generally believed that it was so called because it was usually stowed near the fore sheet: the sheet of the fore sail.

794

on the shelf. The phrase refers to a person *no longer performing one's former activities.* In a shop the goods that are not likely to be asked for or to be saleable are stored on shelves at the back, away from the main stock that is in the window or is easily got at. The phrase used to be applied to a woman who through being elderly or otherwise unattractive, was unlikely to have proposals of marriage.

795

dead men's shoes: see 217.

796

in a person's shoes. *in the same circumstances as those of a given person:* e.g. 'I should not like to be in his shoes', or 'I wish I were in his shoes'. 'shoes', in which a person literally stands, is a natural figure to use for the circumstances in which figuratively he stands.

797

on a shoe-string. (S) *on the price of a shoe-string: on extremely little money.* The phrase comes from U.S.A. 'shoe-lace' was a century later than 'shoe-string', which here in ordinary usage is obsolete.

798

That is another pair of shoes. *That is quite another matter, consideration, set of circumstances, situation.* 'shoes' may have been chosen by the inventor of the metaphor because two pairs can look much like one another, yet be extremely different in their fit and comfort; or the given matter and its circumstances may have been personified as a person standing in shoes.

799

where the shoe pinches. *the circumstance that is the cause of trouble.* A shoe may fit comfortably except at one spot. The expression goes back as far as Chaucer, in a description of a man unhappily married, though he affected cheerfulness.

For god it woot, he sat ful ofte and song
Whan that his shoo ful bitterly him wrong.

800

shoot one's bolt. *do all one can do; use one's last resource.* The expression is nearly always applied to a person who has done this. A 'bolt' was the short heavy arrow of the cross-bow.

801

short-circuit. In its figurative use to 'short-circuit' means, in dealing with official and business affairs, to *irregularly address one's enquiries etc. direct to a person or department* without letting them go through the usual and longer procedure. In its technical use a short-circuit is a deflecting of an electric current along a short route, which often causes the wire to fuse.

802

short shrift. 'shrift' meant primarily confession to, or confession to and absolution from, a priest. The word is now obsolete except in this phrase 'short shrift', which strictly means 'little time between condemnation and execution or other punishment'.

803

a show-down. *C.O.D.* defines the term, in its figurative use, as a 'final test, disclosure of achievements or possibilities', but the word has recently come into frequent use as a synonym of 'trial of strength', or even for a private 'row'.

804

show one's face: see 314.

805

show one's hand: see 400.

806

show one's teeth. *take a threatening tone, or show by threatening word or action one's desire or intention to injure.* The metaphor is that of an animal: e.g. a dog, which uncovers the teeth by withdrawing the lips from them.

807

show the cloven hoof. *betray something evil or sinister in one's character or aims.* The allusion is to the representation of the Devil as being unable, even when otherwise in human shape, to divest himself of cloven hoofs. In the Bible the Devil is a serpent, and, after he has brought about the fall of man in Eden, God condemns him, as a punishment, for ever to remain one. But by the Rabbinical writers he is called *seirizzim*, a goat, as a type of uncleanness: hence his representation with a cloven foot.

808

shut (or **slam**) **the door.** *decisively reject a proposal, or put an end to further discussion.* A door is shut behind a person when he is dismissed, or against a caller: e.g. a hawker whom one refuses to listen to.

809

.. **sign on the dotted line.** *do exactly what one is told; follow instructions in the smallest particulars; accept without demur conditions put before one.* The metaphor is taken from a printed form in which there is a space, marked by dots, for a person's signature.

Compare **toe the line** (418).

810

sing a different tune. *assume a different attitude; behave in a different way.* That a person will sing a different tune in this sense generally implies that he will be forced to do so

811

sink or swim. *fail or succeed.* The phrase is generally used in such a statement as 'He must sink or swim', or 'It is a case of sink or swim', meaning 'He will fail unless he manages by his own efforts to succeed'. 'It was suggested that the United Nations might decide to withdraw their forces from Korea, and leave the South Koreans to sink or swim.'

812

a Sisyphean task. *an endless and fruitless task.* Sisyphus was a King of Corinth, notable for cruelty and rapine. After death he was condemned by Zeus to roll a huge boulder up a high mountain, which, every time it reached the summit, fell back again to the bottom.

813

sit on the fence. *in discussion, politics etc., refrain from committing oneself to either side.* A person is imagined as sitting on a fence separating two properties, and not in either of them. The expression came from U.S.A., where fences take the place of English hedges. Compare **come down on the right side of the fence** (165).

814

It is six of one and half a dozen of the other. *The difference between the two people or things is only nominal.*

815

at sixes and sevens. *in confusion or in disagreement.* The current meaning of the phrase is simple and well established, but its origin and development must be as complicated as those of any idiom in the language. The phrase, says *O.E.D.*, was based on the language of dicing.

It denoted at first the hazarding of one's whole fortune, or carelessness about the consequences of one's actions; and only later the creation of, or existence of, or neglect to remove, disorder or disagreement. *O.E.D.* considers that in its original form the expression did not contain the words 'sixes and sevens' but was 'to set (= 'lay') on *cinque* and *six* (French 'five' and 'six')', the two highest numbers in dicing; and that 'sixes and sevens' was a fanciful alteration, with, later, 'on' turned into 'at'.

816

skate on thin ice. *take part in an affair in which there is extreme danger of failure and disaster.*

817

a skeleton in the cupboard. *a source of shame, especially to the members of a family, that is kept secret.*

818

slap-dash (or **slapdash** or **slap dash**). As *S.O.E.D.* defines it: *in a hasty, sudden, or precipitate manner, especially without much consideration, thought, ceremony, or care.* What a jolly onomatopoeic word, with its vivid picture of a person, in action or words, slapping and dashing his way along !

819

sleep like a top. *sleep soundly.* When a top is spinning it appears motionless. Children talk about a top 'sleeping'.

820

sleep on the matter. *allow a night to pass before reaching a decision.*

821

slip through one's fingers: see 344.

822

small beer. *trivial matters.* Cf. *Othello*, II, i, 149: 'suckle fools and chronicle small beer'. Literally, 'small beer' was a term applied to beer that was weak, mild. The term is often used in the expression 'think no small beer' = 'have a high opinion'.

823

small fry. *unimportant, insignificant people.* 'fry', literally, is the young of animals produced in large numbers, especially fish, but also of bees, frogs, etc. Figuratively the word is applied, as well as to unimportant, insignificant grown-ups, to children: e.g. 'The small fry of the household were then sent up to bed'.

824

the small hours. *the early hours in the morning:* 'small' because they are indicated by small numbers, from 1 to 4 or 5, as contrasted with those when as a rule people begin the day's work.

825

There's no smoke without fire. *Widespread rumours mean that there must be some substance of fact behind them.*

826

a snake in the grass. *a treacherous or dangerous person.* 'in the grass' = (literally) 'hiding in the grass': i.e. figuratively, not an open, but a hidden, enemy. Chaucer in *The Somnours Tale* (l. 1994) has

> War fro the serpent that so slyly crepeth
> Under the grass, and stingeth subtilly.

The first record of the phrase as now established is in 1696, when Charles Leslie, the non-juror controversialist, used it for the title of a pamphlet.

827

snap one's fingers: see 345.

828

So long! *Good-bye!* As Mr. Ivor Brown points out in *A Word in Edgeways*, the origin of the phrase 'So long' meaning 'Good-bye' is obscure. He describes it as less melancholy than 'Farewell' (now rather archaic); less confident than 'Au revoir' (French = 'Until we see one another again'); less optimistic than 'Cheerio'. He might have added that it was less serious than 'Good-bye' (which is a corruption of 'God be with you'). He suggests that it may have developed from 'So long as', and may therefore be a combination of an elision with an attempt to convey the meaning of 'Au revoir': 'Good luck for so long as we are parted and until we see one another again'.

829

up to snuff. *knowing, sharp, not childishly ignorant or innocent.* The original allusion was probably to a person who was mature enough to take snuff (which at one time was more common than tobacco). The earliest record of the expression cited by the *Oxford Book of English Proverbs* is in 1811. (OO)

830

soft soap. *flattery.* 'soft soap', literally, is soap made with potassium remaining liquid, and easy to smear over surfaces to be washed. For the use of 'soap' to mean 'flattery' compare the phrase 'flattering unction' in *Hamlet* (III, iv, 145), though there the 'flattery' is what a person administers to his conscience or self-esteem.

831

sold a pup. (S) *cheated, swindled.* The phrase was probably invented to mean the sale of a dog, supposed to be pure-bred with a pedigree, that was a mongrel.

832

something in the wind. To state that there is **something in the wind** means one infers from signs or evidence something is about to happen. The allusion is to a sailor sensing a change of weather.

833

for a song. *extremely cheap.* The expression is used of buying and selling, especially of buying. Possibly it refers to the time when, before the existence of professional singers, a song cost nothing; or to the small price at which songs used to be hawked.

834

a sop to Cerberus. *something given or done that will mollify, persuade, or bribe, a person whom one wishes to persuade to tolerate some proposed action.* Cerberus was the many-headed dog in classical mythology that guarded Hades, preventing the living from entering the realms of Pluto, and the dead from leaving them. In Virgil's *Aeneid,* when a living person, the Sibyl, visited Hades, she threw a medicated cake (a 'sop') to Cerberus, who ate it and fell asleep, so allowing the visitor to pass.

835

sound as a bell. *perfectly sound in body, or mind, or both.* A bell, if it is to perform its function properly, must be perfectly whole without any crack or other fault.

836

sounding brass. *mere words and noise without sense.* The term comes from the Bible (I *Corinthians,* 13, 1): 'Though I speak with the tongues of men and of angels, and have not charity, I am become as sounding brass, or a tinkling cymbal'.

837

in the soup. *in serious difficulties.* (OO)

838

sour grapes. 'It is a case of sour grapes' means that a person disparages as worthless something that he is unable to get. The allusion is to a fable of Aesop in which a fox having tried in vain to reach some grapes goes away saying they are sour.

839

sow one's wild oats. *commit youthful indiscretions and follies:* usually with the implication of subsequent reform on settling down. (I have not come across the phrase applied to women, though today there is not a male monopoly of the practice.) The allusion is to the sowing of wild species of *Avena*, some of which are indigenous to this country, especially the Wild Oat, *Avena fatua*, instead of good cultivated grain. The phrase is recorded as used as far back as the later part of the seventeenth century.

840

sow the wind and reap the whirlwind. *pay the penalty for causing turmoil by suffering evils infinitely worse.*

841

speak by the card. *be precise to a small point.* The phrase originated in *Hamlet*, V, i: 'How absolute the knave is! we must speak by the card, or equivocation will undo us'. Brewer says that the phrase may refer to documents containing written instructions, but considers, in view of the use of the word 'card' shortly afterwards in the play (V, ii), that more probably the reference is to the points of the compass on a card. Compare also *Macbeth*, I, iii, 16:

> All the quarters that they know
> I' the shipman's card.

'card' and 'chart' are both derived from the Latin *charta* or *carta* = 'papyrus plant'; then 'paper'; then 'a writing'.

842

speak with (or **have**) **one's tongue in one's cheek.** *not to say sincerely and openly what one thinks or means.*

843

spick and span (or spick and span new). *perfectly, wholly, new.* Today the shorter form is commoner. 'spick' = 'neat', 'trim', 'smart', goes back to the seventeenth century. 'span' comes from an Old Norse word meaning 'new'. The early form of the expression contained only the words 'span new'. It so appears, spelt in one word, 'spannewe', as far back as the fourteenth century in *The Lay of Havelock the Dane*, and Chaucer has it in *Troilus and Criseyde*. Later came 'spick and span new'. The first record of 'spick and span' is in Pepys's *Diary*, 1665.

844

spike a person's guns. *by sudden and drastic action prevent a person carrying out his plans or pursuing his activities.* Guns used to be put out of action by driving an iron spike into the touch-hole.

845

split hairs: see 469.

846

split the difference. *halve the amount in dispute.* A considers he is owed £10 by B. B considers his debt is only £6. The difference is £4. Half of £4 is £2. A agrees to accept £10 less £2, and B to give £6 plus £2: i.e. the debt is compounded.

847

spoil the Egyptians. *force your enemies to supply your needs.* The phrase comes from the Bible, where (*Exodus*, 3, 22; 12, 36), as Moses was assured by God, the Egyptians lent the Israelites things they needed.

848

spoil the ship for a ha'porth of tar. *cause a transaction etc. to fail by economy on a small item.* The phrase was originally 'spoil the sheep', and came from the operation of tarring animals, against flies, or as ointment for the treatment of sores caused by them. The *Oxford Book of English Proverbs* states that in many parts of England 'sheep' is dialectically pronounced 'ship'. In the early forms of the expression, for the use of which there are records as far back as the early part of the seventeenth century, there are variants from 'sheep', of 'ewe' and 'hog', and, from 'spoil', of 'lose'.

849

sponge on. *habitually take advantage of a person's good nature to get money or other benefits from him.* The 'sponger' extracts these as a sponge sucks up water.

850

a sprat to catch a mackerel. *a small unimportant sacrifice, as a present, in expenditure of money, in an investment, or even in an amount of work undertaken, with the aim of* *gaining something important and valuable in return.* Presumably the original meaning of the phrase was that it would be worth while to use a small and cheap fish like a sprat as bait to catch a larger and more valuable fish like a mackerel.

851

up the spout. (S) *in pawn; at a pawnbroker's shop.* Thirty or forty years ago this was a familiar slang phrase with reference to a person who was obliged to resort to the unfortunate necessity of pawning a possession at a pawnbroker's shop (in other slang phrases, 'popping it', 'putting it into pop'). The 'spout' was a sloping trough, for shooting pawned objects into a receptacle. The expression in this sense is now unfamiliar except to the elderly. Today 'up the spout' is used, if at all, as a slang term, with reference to a person or a firm in financial difficulties or bankrupt.

852

spread like wildfire. The phrase is always used with reference to rumours, news, etc. 'wildfire', or 'Greek fire', is a combustible composition for setting on fire enemy's ships, etc.

SQUARE

There is a large number of idioms introducing the word 'square', as noun, adjective, adverb, and verb. A mathematical friend, disclaiming, as their origin, theoretical geometry, thinks it was probably carpentering and building.

Squareness, in its usual meaning of 'four-equal-sidedness', suggests regularity. A figurative extension of this is correctness, straightness, rightness. A link between the literal and figurative meanings can be seen in the term 'right angle'. Compare, too, for the opposite of figurative straightness, the figurative use of crookedness. A dishonest person and dishonest behaviour are often said to be crooked. But the figurative extensions are often rather remote from the primary sense.

853

be on the square. *act honestly and straightforwardly.*

854

a round peg in a square hole (or **a square peg in a round hole**). *a person who, though he may have abilities, is in a position that is unsuited and uncongenial to him.* Compare **a fish out of water** (347).

855

a square (or **fair and square**) **deal.** *an honest and straightforward transaction.*

856

a square meal is *a full meal.*

857

four square means *solidly based* (literally and figuratively). It is often used to qualify the verb 'to stand'. 'four' is pleonastic, because a square is essentially four-sided.

858

get a matter square. *arrange it so that it is fair to all sides.*

859

It is all square: see 15.

860

We will call it square. *We regard it as settled fairly.* There is sometimes also an implication that the speaker or speakers agree to make no further claims.

861

hit square (or squarely). *hit right, exactly, on the effective spot:* e.g. 'He hit him square on the jaw'; or, figuratively, in argument, etc., *make an effective point.*

862

play square (or squarely). *act fairly.*

863

square a person. *gain a person's agreement, consent, in return for what lawyers call a consideration, financial or moral.* Sometimes in a bad sense it means to bribe him.

864

square an account. *have an account, a charge, settled and paid.*

865

square accounts (plural) has another meaning, of *have revenge.*

866

to square the circle, meaning *to attempt the impossible,* has a mathematical origin. As the ratio between the diameter and the circumference of a circle cannot be determined precisely, it is impossible to construct a square of the same area as that of a given circle.

867

square up. *settle a matter by paying.*

868

square with. *make* or *be consistent with.*

869

make one's hair stand on end: see 284.

870

not a leg to stand on: see 629.

871

stand in a person's light. *act in such a way as to spoil a person's chance of benefiting, especially from an opportunity in his career.* Literally A stands casting a shadow on B's work.

There is also the expression **stand in one's own light,** meaning to spoil one's own chance. Here the person concerned is conceived as standing in such a position that he prevents himself from getting the light that otherwise might come to him.

872

stand on one's own feet (or **legs**)**:** see 370.

873

stand in a white sheet. *confess one's errors in a humble spirit.* In former days a sinner who publicly expressed penitence wore a white sheet.

874

His star was in the ascendant. *His success, power, importance, fortunes, etc., were increasing.* This idiom combines a metaphor from astronomy: of a star that rises in the sky, with one from astrology: of a star considered as influencing a person's career. Compare **thank one's stars** (935) and **His star was set.**

875

stay put: see 712.

876

steal a march on. *gain a secret advantage over a rival or opponent.* The allusion is military, referring to success in moving soldiers without the knowledge of the enemy.

877

steal a person's thunder. *make use of literary devices, arguments, etc., taken from another speaker or writer, as one's own:* i.e. plagiarise. The origin of the phrase is commonly ascribed to the dramatist and critic John Dennis (1657–1734), with reference to a new form of metallic arrangement for imitating thunder on the stage. When one of his plays was a failure he bitterly complained that the management had withdrawn it but in another production had 'stolen the thunder'.

In the fifth century A.D. a Greek epic poet Nonnos told a story of how, when Zeus had hidden his thunderbolts in a cave, a monster Typhoeus stole them, and Zeus had to resort to a stratagem in order to recover them; and Milton, who had perhaps read Nonnos, attributes in *Paradise Lost* the victory of God over Satan and the other rebellious angels to the superior force of the thunderbolts used against them. But it is improbable that an allusion to Nonnos, whose work is not well known, could have got into the English language as the source of the phrase.

For the gist of the matter in this note I am indebted to Professor H. J. Rose and Professor W. S. Watt.

878

out of step. (a person, policy, act, thought, etc.) *not agreeing, not in accord, with some other person, policy, etc., referred to.* The metaphor is from military drill.

879

step off on the wrong foot: see 371.

880

stew (or fry) in his own juice. *suffer the results of difficulties he has got into.* The phrase dates to 1656.

881

stick to one's guns. *in spite of all arguments against one, remain firmly constant to one's opinions and principles*, as an artilleryman does to his gun however heavily attacked.

882

to stomach. *to tolerate.* The verb is generally used only negatively. The use of *stomach* as a noun, for the seat of digestion of food, goes back to late Middle English. When it came into use as a verb, it was only figuratively, with its present meaning of 'tolerate', 'endure', 'put up with'. It was not until a century later that *S.O.E.D.* cites its use literally, and with a meaning exactly opposite to this: of 'turn the stomach'. Then, shortly afterwards, it was used, intransitively, to mean 'take offence', 'feel resentment'. One word in its time plays many parts.

883

a storm in a teacup. *a lot of fuss about a trifle*, especially in a circumscribed circle of people. Mr. Eric Partridge cites similar expressions: 'a storm in a cream-bowl' (1678), 'a storm in a wash-hand basin' (1830). *O.E.D.* says that the origin of the phrase is probably an expression by Cicero in *de Legibus: fluctus excitare in simpulo:* 'to stir up waves in a ladle'.

884

straight from the horse's mouth. *information direct from reliable sources.* A horse is conceived as knowing which will be the winner in a coming race, or at all events the part he will take in it, and as giving a tip about this to a person betting in the race.

885

straight from the shoulder. (saying something, or having something said, to a person, attacking him, reprimanding him, etc.) *in a direct, outspoken, blunt way.* The metaphor is from boxing.

886

a straight tip. A 'tip' by itself can mean *a friendly hint, or a piece of useful private or special information communicated by an expert,* used especially for advice about betting or a Stock Exchange speculation intended to benefit the recipient (*S.O.E.D.*). A 'straight' tip is such information as is correct, and coming direct from a person with expert knowledge.

887

strain at a gnat (often followed by **and swallow a camel**). *demur over a small matter while acquiescing in much more important matters.* The phrase is found in the Bible (*Matthew*, 23, 24). The Authorised Version has 'Ye blind guides which strain at a gnat and swallow a camel'. *C.O.D.* gives 'strain' here as meaning 'be over-scrupulous'. The Revised Version has, instead of 'strain at a gnat', 'strain out the gnat', where 'strain' means to clear liquid of solid matter by a sieve or other strainer; but the current form of the expression has retained 'strain at'.

888

up my street. (S) The phrase is used (often with **right up**) for a matter regarded as falling or not falling within one's knowledge or experience, or being what one could or could not easily and satisfactorily deal with. The allusion is to the sort of thing that would happen in the street where one lives; and by extension the expression has come to be applied to the sort of thing that does or does not enter into one's mental or practical experience. Compare **one's line of country** (558).

889

streets ahead. *far in advance; much superior.* The superiority of a person or thing is regarded as measured by not the distance of a few inches or feet, but the length of several streets.

890

stretch (or **strain**) **a point.** *S.O.E.D.* gives two meanings of these phrases. (1) *do more than one is bound to do.* An example would be that of an employer who in special circumstances allows a clerk a day's extra holiday. (2) *go further in a matter than one is entitled.* 'Fowler strains a point when he states that in the English language it is doubtful whether any perfect synonyms exist.' The connecting link between the words of the phrases and their current figurative meanings is that a thing is extended to a point beyond its ordinary limits.

891

strike oil. *attain sudden and great success in becoming rich.* Literally the phrase, from U.S.A., means to reach petroleum by sinking a shaft. It is supposed to have been introduced here by Sir Walter Besant in his novel *The Golden Butterfly* (1876).

892

Strike while the iron is hot. *Take advantage of favourable circumstances to act at once, when action will have the most effect.* The allusion is to a blacksmith's forge, where a horseshoe or other object must be hammered into shape while it is hot. Compare **make hay while the sun shines** (580) and **take time by the forelock** (910).

Chaucer in *Troilus and Criseyde* (II, 1275) has, in a metaphorical use,

> Pandare, which that stood hir faste by,
> Felte iren hoot, and he began to smyte.

Two centuries later John Heywood has

> And one good lesson to this purpose I pike
> From the smithis forge, when thyron is hot strike.

Bunyan uses the expression metaphorically, as does Shakespeare in several plays: e.g. *III Henry VI*, V, 1, 49:

> Strike now, or else the iron cools.

893

That's the stuff to give him (her, them). *That's what to do* (especially the strong language to use: originally **the stuff to give the troops**, to raise their spirits).

894

sub rosa. *in secrecy, in strict confidence. sub rosa* is Latin for 'under the rose'. The origin of the connection between the rose and secrecy is obscure. The phrase *sub rosa* with this connotation does not occur in ancient literature. In an edition of Virgil, published at Madrid early in the seventeenth century, the editor, J. L. de la Cerda, quotes a Latin epigram that describes Cupid giving a rose to Harpocrates, the god of silence, to bribe him not to betray the amours of Venus. La Cerda adds that it was a custom among Germans of his time to hang a rose, or a symbol of a rose, in the dining-rooms of inns, to remind the diners that what was said and done there should not be divulged. H. Meyer in an anthology of Latin poems and epigrams (Leipzig, 1835) suggests that the epigram was concocted in order to explain the origin of the phrase, and *O.E.D.* says that the phrase may have originated in Germany.

The earliest example given by *O.E.D.* of *sub rosa* is 1654; of the vernacular phrase, 'under the rose', a century earlier (1546). In Germany the phrase *unter der Rosen* is stated to have been common from the fifteenth to the seventeenth centuries. The Germans have also the phrase *unter der Blume* ('under the flower') with the same connotation of secrecy.

I am greatly indebted for the information contained in this note to Professor W. S. Watt.

895

swan song. *the last literary or musical production of a person, especially one composed shortly before his death.* The allusion is to the fabulous belief that a swan sings shortly or immediately before it dies. Cicero expressed the belief in his *Tusculan Disputations.* There the swan is a pessimist that 'foreseeing how much good there is in death, dies with song and rejoicing'. Chaucer, John Lydgate (1430), Sir Thomas Browne (1650), refer to the belief; and Shakespeare: e.g. *Othello*, V, ii, 245.

896

swing the lead. The figurative slang meaning is *exaggerate, tell a tall story, malinger* (pretend to be ill in order to avoid work). This is all that can be said with certainty about a phrase of which the origin is obscure.

O.E.D. under 'swing' enters the phrase only in the senses given above: i.e. the figurative senses, and not in any literal sense. Under 'lead' on the other hand it does not give 'swing the lead', but 'heave the lead' and 'cast the lead', in only the literal sense, for the nautical process of throwing into the water, to find its depth, a piece of lead, a plummet, attached to a line.

So much for the dictionary. The son of a friend of mine who served in the Navy in the last war says that he always heard the nautical process called, not 'heaving' or 'casting', but 'swinging', the lead.

Mr. Eric Partridge in his *Dictionary of Slang* says that 'swing the lead' is a perversion of a nautical phrase 'swing the leg', which meant to 'malinger'. (One can imagine how a malingering sailor might be described as sitting about, swinging his legs, instead of using them to go about his duties.) He adds that this corruption was introduced by soldiers who erroneously imagined that the taking of soundings, which is an arduous and a skilful duty, was easy, and admitted of loafing.

Against all this a person known to me, who fifty years ago voyaged in sailing ships, became a Commander in the Navy, and is a Brother of Trinity House, says he never knew the phrase 'swing the leg' all the years he was at sea; and from yet another source, not nautical, but well-informed, I am told that taking soundings is an operation that physically is an easy job compared, for example, with swabbing the deck; that it was often given to those who were not well or strong; that sometimes men would pretend they were not well so that they might be given the job, and that from this came the association of the phrase with malingering.

Here this complicated matter must remain.

897

the sword of Damocles. *imminent danger in the midst of prosperity.* The allusion is to the story of a Greek courtier, who having flattered Dionysius, King of Syracuse (fourth century B.C.), by extolling his happiness, was placed by him at a banquet with a sword suspended over his head by a hair, to impress upon him how precarious happiness was.

898

to a T. *exactly, to a nicety.* 'T' means a 'T-square', a T-shaped instrument for getting or testing right angles.

899

take a person down a peg. *lower a person's conceit.* The origin of the phrase was in the old seafaring practice of rendering honours by hoisting a ship's flag. This was originally done by pegs that were raised according to the rank of the person to be honoured, and that could similarly be lowered if in the process of doing this it was found that they had been raised too high.

900

take French leave. *go away, be absent, or do a thing, without permission or without notice. S.O.E.D.* says 'French leave' originally referred to the custom, prevalent in the seventeenth century in France, of going away from a reception etc. without taking leave of the host or hostess. Then jocularly it came to mean to do anything without permission or notice. The French have the same meaning in the phrase *filer à l'anglaise* = 'to go off in English style'. It looks as if each nation ascribed bad manners to its hereditary enemy. There are also other uncomplimentary things that the French said were English, and the English said were French.

901

take in one's stride. *In going about one's ordinary activities, or a particular one, automatically effect a secondary purpose.* The metaphor is that of a person whose feet, as he walks to his destination, pass over, without his thinking of it, everything on the ground.

902

take off one's hat to. *feel great respect and admiration for.*

903

take pot luck: see 680.

904

take the bit between one's teeth. *throw off control.* The allusion is to a horse, which is controlled by the pressure of the bit (the mouthpiece of the bridle) on the soft part of its mouth. If the horse succeeds in getting this between the teeth, the rider or driver has not the same control of it.

905

take the bull by the horns. *boldly face and tackle the difficulty.* Compare **take the wolf by the ears** (1003).

906

take the gilt off the gingerbread. *deprive a situation or circumstance of an advantage whose loss leaves it without any attraction.* The allusion is to gingerbread cakes in the shape of men, animals, etc., decorated with gold leaf, that used to be sold at fairs. When the gilt decoration, by age or handling, was worn off, the gingerbread no longer looked inviting.

907

take (or **carry**) **the can.** (S) *shoulder blame for something one was not responsible for.* 'I am not going to take the can for that.' The metaphor is an army one. I hear from a military informant that in the development of the present meaning of the expression the idea of responsibility (though not that of being wrongly held responsible) was probably connected with the duty of a soldier to return to the depot empty tins when the contents: e.g. tea, jam, petrol, had been used.

908

take the cake (or **biscuit**). Originally 'take the cake' referred to the prize awarded to the pair of negroes who in a competition were adjudged to have walked most gracefully round a cake. From this there evolved a dance that early in the present century became popular. Today the phrase is used only ironically with reference to some action or statement that *wins first prize*, or *takes the record*, for being foolish, absurd, outrageous. There is also the expression, not used so much, 'takes the biscuit'.

909

take the shine out of. *make appear inferior and insignificant*. The metaphor is that of a strong and brilliant light causing a lesser one to become inconspicuous: as e.g. bright sunshine dulls the glow of a fire.

910

take time by the forelock. *act promptly*. There is often a further implication, of seizing a favourable opportunity: compare **make hay while the sun shines** (580) and **Strike while the iron is hot** (892). 'Time', says Swift, 'is painted with a lock before, and bald behind; signifying thereby, that we must take time by the *forelock*; for when it is once past there is no recalling it.' The Greek god of Occasion, Chairos, was represented with a full forelock. In English literature the allusion appears as far back as in 1591, in Robert Greene's *Farewell to Folly*: 'Take time now by the forehead: she is bald behinde'. Shakespeare, who uses the image in several plays, calls Time 'that bald sexton' (*King John*, III, i, 324).

911

take to task. *blame, call to account, about a matter*. The noun 'task' here is used in the sense of 'blame' in the same way in which the verb 'to task' was used to mean 'to blame', but is now obsolete in that sense except in this phrase.

912

take the wind out of a person's sails. *frustrate a person's efforts.* A ship that goes close to windward of another robs it of the wind it needs for its sails.

913

take with a grain of salt. *regard* (a statement, story, etc.) *as not wholly true.* If the English phrase is, as has been stated without evidence, a translation of a Latin phrase *cum grano salis*, that probably comes from medieval Latin, for I learn from Professor W. S. Watt that in classical Latin the word for salt was never used figuratively with the sense of 'disbelief'.

914

talk a person's head off: see 504.

915

talk nineteen to the dozen. *speak so quickly as not to give a chance to others to get a word in edgeways.* The speaker is described as using nineteen words when a dozen would do. Why 'nineteen'? The obvious numeral would be the round number 'twenty'. Possibly 'nineteen' was chosen just because, not being what might have been expected, it seemed to give a more striking effect.

916

talk shop. *discuss one's business or professional affairs on ordinary social occasions.*

917

talk through his hat. *exaggerate or invent.* The origin is unknown but compare 'tall' for an improbable story, and 'high-faluting' (513).

918

tarred with the same brush: see 760.

919

by the skin of one's teeth. *barely, only just.* The phrase always refers to a narrow escape. The shortness of the distance separating a person from the disaster he has escaped is compared to the thinness of the skin round the teeth. The expression is in the Bible: *Job*, 19, 20: 'I am escaped with the skin of my teeth'. ('by' is a popular error.)

920

cast (or **throw** or **fling**) **in a person's teeth:** see 125.

921

get one's teeth into. *become closely engaged in* (an undertaking). The image may be that of a person who is eating something, or of an animal, e.g. a dog, fighting with another.

922

in the teeth of. This idiom has several uses with slightly different shades of meaning that are shown by the context in which it appears. The meanings of the phrase are: (1) *in direct opposition to;* (2) *in defiance of;* (3) *in the presence of;* (4) *threateningly faced by;* (5) *in spite of.* That which is metaphorically confronted etc. is generally an order, rule, instruction; but it may be a physical thing: e.g. 'We decided to press on in the teeth of the piercing wind.' The allusion is to being threateningly confronted by an animal showing its teeth.

923

set one's teeth on edge: see 787.

924

show one's teeth: see 806.

925

take the bit between one's teeth: see 904.

926

tooth and nail. *vigorously*, *fiercely*. (The form was originally 'with tooth and nail' = 'using teeth to bite with and nails to scratch with'.) The phrase is nearly always used figuratively, and often with 'went for' (him or her), for blaming a person for something.

927

A little bird told me: see 563.

928

tell (a person) flat. 'flat' (strictly an adjective) is here used as an adverb ('flatly'). It means *frankly*, *openly*, *straight out*, *without mincing matters* (605), or (if, as recommended in *The Choice of Words*, that word is not to be banished from the vocabulary) *definitely*.

Similarly we 'flatly' 'say, refuse, deny, contradict', etc.; and we have a 'flat refusal, denial, contradiction', etc. The link between the primary meaning of 'flat': i.e. 'horizontally level', and the meaning of the idiom seems to be that, whereas in ordinary communications between people, language has adornments, decorations, qualifications, euphemisms, restraints within the bounds of politeness, here in e.g. 'flatly refusing', 'a flat refusal', the expression is, as it were, flattened out, so that there are no curves, projections, creases, etc., to break up, hide, soften, the bare outline of a positive, categorical statement.

929

tell a person off. (S) *speak sharply to a person in reproof, blame, complaint.* The connection between the 'tell' and 'off' with the meaning of the phrase is obscure. *S.O.E.D.*, entering it as 'slang', meaning 'scold', 'rebuke strongly', includes it among the phrases related to 'tell' in its sense of 'mention numerically', 'count', 'reckon'. Perhaps the underlying idea is that of enumerating a list of offences complained of.

930

tell tales out of school. *divulge secrets that came to one's knowledge from confidential sources.* The phrase appears in Heywood's *Proverbs* in 1546.

931

Tell that to the marines. *Nonsense!* The expression was originally 'Tell that to the horse marines', meaning 'The only people to believe that are the horse marines, who do not exist'. The phrase no doubt owed its popularity (especially about 1870) to the amusingly absurd image of a body of soldiers serving on ships as cavalry, with horses.

932

You are telling me. (S) *As if I did not know.* The phrase cannot be explained so as to show how it came to have its meaning unless we imagine that it is an ellipsis for 'You are telling me what I knew already'.

933

temper the wind to the shorn lamb. *adopt gentle methods in dealing with the weaker brethren.* 'temper' here means 'regulate', 'restrain', 'check', 'curb', so as to prevent the animal from being exposed to cold winds: as a lamb just shorn is more susceptible to cold than a full-grown sheep. The original proverb seems to have been French, in which language it is found as far back as the end of the sixteenth century in 'Dieu mesure le froid ['the cold', instead of 'the wind'] à la brebis tondue'. George Herbert in his collection of proverbs (1640) cites it as 'To a close shorn lamb God gives wind by measure'. Sterne in *A Sentimental Journey* has '"God tempers the wind", said Maria, "to the shorn lamb"'.

934

on tenterhooks. *in a state of painful suspense or impatient uncertainty.* A 'tenter' was originally a frame used for stretching cloth. The cloth was attached to the frame by hooks such as are found in butchers' shops for hanging meat, and the frame was adjusted to the requisite tightness. In the Middle Ages prisoners were impaled on tenterhooks. They were suspended on the hooks by the chin, and the weight of the body forced the point of the hook through the lower jaw into the mouth and tongue. Hence came the figurative extension of the phrase 'stretched on tenter-hooks'.

935

thank (or **bless**) **one's stars** (or **lucky stars**). *recognise how fortunate one has been in the circumstances.* The metaphor is from astrology, according to which the stars influence our fortunes. Compare **His star was in the ascendant** (874), and **to be born under a lucky star.**

936

the thin end of the wedge: see 288.

937

a thorn in the flesh. *a small trouble that nevertheless is a constant irritation.* The Bible has several passages where a thorn is used figuratively: 'pricks in your eyes and thorns in your sides' (*Numbers*, 33, 55); 'thorns in your sides' (*Judges*, 2, 3); and 'a thorn in the flesh' appears in II *Corinthians*, 12, 7.

938

throw a spanner in the works. *disturb the execution of a plan, operation, etc.* A spanner thrown into machinery would upset its working.

939

throw down the gauntlet. *challenge.* This use of 'gauntlet' is derived from the French word *gantelot*, meaning 'glove', and originated in the Middle Ages, when a knight issued a challenge by throwing down his armoured glove. 'gauntlet' is still used today, apart from this idiom, for a stout glove with long wrist, for driving, fencing, etc.

940

throw dust in a person's eyes: see 297.

941

throw good money after bad: see 458.

942

throw her bonnet (or cap) over the windmill. *commit herself to a love affair without reserve or regard to conventions.* 'bonnet' and 'cap' seem to be regarded as emblems of respectability. 'over the windmill' may imply being cast away irretrievably over the whirling sails. Compare the idiom 'throw to the winds', especially 'throw discretion to the winds'. The wind is often used as a symbol of a rude force that is indifferent to convention and propriety. 'The wind bloweth where it listeth' (*John*, 3, 8). Dr. Sydney Cole, in a letter to me, suggests that the young woman of the idiom throws off her bonnet to show an open and unashamed face. Mrs. Nancy Henry, to whom I owe much of this note, adds that a bonnet or cap, apart from its being an emblem of respectability, is a protective covering, and that to throw it away is to be reckless and expose oneself to rain and wind and cold, and, figuratively, to social penalties.

943

throw (or **cast** or **fling**) **in a person's teeth:** see 125.

944

throw to the wolves. *sacrifice, give as a sop:* i.e. in order to extricate oneself from a difficult situation, or pacify opponents or critics, one sacrifices a subordinate person who is not primarily or seriously guilty in the matter concerned, so making him a sort of scapegoat. Perhaps the idea underlying the expression is that of throwing food or a living animal to a pack of pursuing wolves in order to divert their attention.

945

throw up the sponge. *give up; not continue a contest.* This is a metaphor from the boxing ring. When a boxer's second tosses a sponge into the air it means that his principal will not enter the next round, and admits he is beaten.

946

thrust down a person's throat. *force on a person's attention* (*an opinion, fact, etc., that is unwelcome*). The metaphor is a figurative application, of the image of a person's being forced literally to swallow something unpleasant, to his being forced to accept something unwelcome to his mind.

947

under the thumb of. *completely subservient to.* See, for a possible origin of this phrase, **turn down** (967).

948

tick a person off. (S) *speak sharply to a person in reproof, blame, complaint. S.O.E.D.*, which says the expression came into use about thirty years ago, enters it, as synonymous with **tell off** (929), among the phrases related to 'tell' in the sense of 'mention numerically', 'count', 'reckon'. The metaphor seems to be that of marking in a list the items of an offender's misdoings.

949

That's the ticket. The phrase is used loosely, with a number of small shades of difference in their meaning = *That's right, satisfactory, good news, the way to do it.*

950

time out of mind. *longer than is known; from time immemorial.* 'mind' = 'memory', in which sense it is now obsolete except in this idiom and a few phrases: 'keep in mind', 'call to mind', 'come to mind', etc.

951

times out of (or **without**) **number.** *extremely often.* 'out of number' is perhaps an elision of 'out of one's power to calculate the number'.

952

on tiptoe. *greatly excited.* Literally one would only stand on the tips of one's toes if one were trying to see over a person or object obstructing the view.

953

tit for tat. *retaliation on an opponent by paying him back in his own coin* (see 656). *C.O.D.* says the phrase may have been originally 'tip for tap'. *S.O.E.D.* gives 'tip' as used in the eighteenth century with the meaning of 'blow'. There is a record of the use of the expression in 1556 in John Heywood's *The Spider and the Flie.*

954

Tom, Dick, and Harry. *the ordinary man.* This expression, which came into use in the Victorian age, comprises the colloquial forms of what were, and probably still are, the most common first-names: Thomas, Richard, and Henry. In *I Henry IV* (II, iv.) Shakespeare has 'Tom, Dick, and Francis'. Today a more common expression is **the man in the street** (588).

955

Tommy Atkins; Tommy. These are popularised forms of 'Thomas Atkins'. *the British common soldier in the ranks; the rank and file:* strictly privates, for corporals and sergeants are 'non-commissioned officers'. The terms have become almost obsolete since the introduction of National Service. Brewer says that the origin of the expression is that at one time recruits were given a manual in which the soldier entered particulars of his name, age, date of enlistment, wounds, medals, and so forth; and that in a specimen form, showing how the one in the manual should be filled in, the hypothetical name used was 'Thomas Atkins'.

Sometimes a soldier in the ranks was described, without 'Atkins', as 'a Tommy'.

956

tommy rot (or **tommyrot**). *utter nonsense.* How a common form of Thomas should have come to be used as an emphasiser of nonsense is obscure. (S)

957

from the top drawer. The phrase is generally used negatively, with reference to a person who is not *born and bred in a good social class:* i.e. not what used to be called a 'lady' or 'gentleman'. If the phrase is used in a positive sense: e.g. 'She comes from the top drawer', the implication would probably be that she belonged to the aristocracy: to what once used to be called 'the upper ten thousand'. The connection between the current meaning of the phrase and the face value of the words is not close. Why is the 'drawer' the 'top' one? Is this because as a rule one's most precious possessions are kept in the top drawer of a chest-of-drawers or desk? A woman friend says this is not so: that, for example, a prospective bride keeps her trousseau in a bottom drawer. Perhaps 'drawer' was taken as a part of a familiar object divided into a top, a middle, and a bottom drawer, corresponding figuratively to what we once dared to call the upper, middle, and lower classes. Or perhaps it was chosen merely for a synonym of 'class' as having a less snobbish air.

958

topsy-turvy. *upside down, with the natural position reversed.* The term is found in print as far back as 1528, and probably its popular use was earlier still. *O.E.D.* says this is no evidence of what the two elements forming this alliterative combination originally were, but that probably 'topsy' represented 'top-side', and probably 'turvy' was connected with 'turve' = 'turn'.

959

a touch of the tar-brush. *C.O.D.* defines this expression as 'an admixture of negro blood as shown by the colour of the skin', but it is sometimes used loosely for an admixture of the blood of other dark-coloured peoples: e.g. Hindus.

960

in touch, e.g. in 'be in touch', 'get into touch', 'come into touch'. *get into relations with.* Pearsall Smith says this use of the word 'touch' probably originated in military drill, where 'touch' meant the contact between the elbows of a rank of soldiers.

961

touch and go: see 455.

962

trail one's coat. *be provocative; give offence deliberately.* Mr. Freeman in his *Concise Dictionary of Idioms* says that to trail or drag one's coat behind one used to be an accepted method of issuing a general challenge: any person stepping on the coat was considered to have insulted its owner; and Mr. Eric Partridge says it was a 'medieval provocation to a duel'. One wonders whether the challenger took his coat off in order to trail it on the ground.

963

tread on a person's corns. *do or say something that will offend a person's prejudices.* The physical action occurs by accident where people are gathered closely together, and the figurative use generally implies that the offence, injury, etc., is not deliberate.

964

Even a worm will turn. *There is a point when even the most subservient and meek person will refuse any longer to submit to his treatment.* There does not seem to be any connection between the meaning of the idiom and the behaviour of the invertebrate creeping animal called a 'worm'. 'turn' = 'turn against (one's opponent)'.

965

not turn a hair: see 467.

966

turn a deaf ear. *refuse to listen*, especially with reference to a person who will not pay any attention to, or entertain the idea of, a request or plea. Many people are deaf in only one ear. The metaphor may be that of a person turning this to the person speaking to him. But the expression may have originated in a biblical allusion to the viper of the Psalms (58, 4): 'They are like the deaf adder that stoppeth her ear; which will not listen to the voice of charmers'. Brewer, in one of his most delightful articles, tells how in the East, if a viper entered a house, a charmer was sent for to entice it into a bag, and that according to tradition, when he uttered his incantation, the snake tried not to hear by putting one ear on the ground, and twisting its tail into the other.

967

turn down. *refuse* (*an application, request, offer, etc.*) *or reject* (*a person making an application, etc.*). Mr. Eric Partridge in his *Dictionary of Slang* says that the meaning of the phrase comes from U.S.A., where the use goes back to the end of the last century. By now it can be regarded as well on its way to becoming established here as literary idiom. *C.O.D.* gives it as a synonym of 'reject'.

A frequently held conjecture that the expression may be connected with 'turn down the thumb (or thumbs)' in reference to a practice by the spectators at shows in the ancient Roman amphitheatre to indicate disapproval of the performance of a gladiator is doubtful.

968

turn one's head: see 505.

969

turn over a new leaf: see 83.

970

turn the tables: see 403.

971

turn up trumps: see 408.

972

twiddle one's thumbs. *sit still doing nothing:* often with the additional idea that one is being forced to waste one's time. Compare **kick one's heels** (535).

973

two bites of or **(at a) cherry.** *two attempts to do something that ought to be done in one.* In French a figurative use of the phrase 'three bites of a cherry' that goes back as far as Rabelais (1548) appeared in an English translation by P. A. Motteux, completing Sir Thomas Urquhart's, in 1693–1694. The earliest record of **two bites at a cherry** is its use in a forgotten novel of 1850.

974

two strings (or **a second string**) **to one's bow.** *a second alternative if one's first attempt fails.* The allusion is to bowmen who in the old days would have with them a second string in case the first snapped.

975

That is up to him. *That is his affair:* i.e. to decide what to do, especially to take the initiative in doing it.

976

on one's uppers. *extremely poor.* The image is that of a person wearing shoes or boots so old that the lower part of the sole has gone, and he is walking on the upper layer of leather. For another metaphor indicating poverty as shown by the state of a person's clothes see **down at heel** (258), here again referring to foot-wear, and **out at elbow** (277).

977

upset the (or **a person's**) **applecart.** *upset the* (*or a person's*) *arrangements.*

978

Use your loaf. (S) *Use your brains* (especially with reference to thinking of some way to get out of a difficulty.) This is chiefly an army phrase. 'loaf' is from rhyming slang: 'loaf of bread': i.e. 'head', with the usual omission of the rhyming word.

I am told that there is, or was, an expression in leap-frog: 'Duck your crust'.

979

with a vengeance. *C.O.D.* defines the phrase as meaning *in a higher degree than was expected or desired; in the fullest sense of the word or words; and no mistake.* All these senses are a long way from the ordinary meaning of 'vengeance'. At best the phrase is a form of asseveration.

980

warm the cockles of one's heart: see 510.

981

wash one's dirty linen in public. *discuss or make public one's grievances, quarrels, conduct that might be thought disreputable.*

982

be on the water wagon. (S) *not indulge in alcoholic drinks; be temporarily teetotal.*

983

wear one's heart on one's sleeve: see 511.

984

under the weather. *depressed or unwell.* 'under' = 'subject to', 'governed by'. The literal meaning would be that one was experiencing bad weather. The figurative meaning is that one's health or spirits are affected by adverse conditions.

985

a wet blanket. *one who by criticism discourages a plan o a person who was feeling cheerful and hopeful about it.* Brewer says that a 'wet blanket' is used to extinguish a fire, but the connection between this action and that connoted in the current meaning of the phrase is at best not close, because a fire that is extinguished is a destructive force. Perhaps the person who first used the phrase figuratively merely regarded the human 'wet blanket' as one who put out a bright flame. But compare the use of the verb 'damp' in such a statement as 'His remarks are rather damping'.

986

wheels within wheels. *a complexity of forces or influences; a complication of motives, designs, plots, etc.* (*S.O.E.D.*). The expression comes from the Bible, in *Ezekiel* (1, 4): 'and their appearance and their work was as it were a wheel in the middle of a wheel'.

987

a white elephant. *a possession that is burdensome in expense or trouble.* The allusion is to a practice kings of Siam were said to have of giving obnoxious courtiers a white elephant in order to ruin them.

988

a whited sepulchre. *one whose behaviour, manner, etc., hide inward badness; a hypocrite.* The phrase comes from the Bible, where (*Matthew*, 23, 16) Jesus rebukes the Scribes and Pharisees as hypocrites 'like unto whited sepulchres, which indeed appear beautiful outward, but are within full of dead men's bones, and of all uncleanness'. 'whited'= 'whitened': the form 'to white' is obsolete. The sepulchres were periodically whitewashed in order that in the dark a passer-by might see them, and his body, by touching them, avoid being defiled. I am indebted for this information to Dr. G. R. Driver.

989

a wild goose chase. *an absurdly hopeless enterprise.* The first record of the expression goes back three and a half centuries to George Chapman. I am indebted to Mr. Peter Scott for the information that geese in their natural state are extremely wild; that until recently their movements have been obscure and unpredictable; that they have been the quarry of men since prehistoric time, but that even now the chase is only rarely successful.

990

win hands down. *win easily.* The metaphor is from horse-racing. A jockey's letting his hands drop in relaxing his hold on the reins means that he is not having to worry himself to make his horse go faster.

991

win his spurs. *gain his reputation.* In medieval times a warrior, when he was knighted for a valiant deed, was given a pair of gold spurs.

992

get (or have) the wind up: see 429.

993

get wind of: see 430.

994

raise the wind: see 721.

995

sail close to the wind: see 755.

996

see how the wind blows: see 778.

997

something in the wind: see 832.

998

sow the wind and reap the whirlwind: see 840.

999

temper the wind to the shorn lamb: see 933.

1000

wipe the floor. (S) *inflict complete and ignominious defeat on an opponent.* The idea in the image seems to be that one's opponent is reduced to such helplessness and inertia that his body is fit only to use as a mop for wiping the floor.

1001

cry wolf. *raise a false alarm.* From Aesop's fable of the shepherd boy who so often cried 'Wolf!' to cause excitement and alarm to his neighbours that, when at last a wolf did come, nobody paid attention, and all the sheep he was in charge of were killed.

1002

keep the wolf from the door. *avoid starvation or acute poverty.* The wolf, as a fierce animal, is taken figuratively as a symbol of destructive force. In days past, when wolves infested the forests and lanes of England, the phrase must have had more significance than it has today. Used figuratively, it appears in John Heywood's collection of proverbs in 1546.

1003

take the wolf by the ears. This means the same as **take the bull by the horns** (see 905), but is naturally less common as wolves no longer exist in Great Britain.

1004

throw to the wolves: see 944.

1005

a wolf in sheep's clothing. *a dangerous enemy who plausibly poses as a friend.* The allusion here is again (compare **cry wolf:** 1001) to a fable of Aesop. A wolf, disguising itself in a sheep's skin, succeeds in deceiving a flock of sheep and entering the sheepfold. There is also a well-known passage in the Bible, in the Sermon on the Mount: 'Beware of false prophets, which come to you in sheep's clothing, but inwardly they are ravening wolves' (*Matthew*, 7, 15).

1006

to wolf. *to eat ravenously*, especially a large portion of food.

1007

wool-gathering. *letting one's thoughts wander vaguely from one thing to another in idle fancies.* Literally the term refers to the action of gathering fragments of wool torn from sheep by hedges etc.: i.e. collecting stray fragments of material that are of little value.

1008

Even a worm will turn: see 964.

1009

not to be worth; not to care. There are a number of words, some slang, that are used with 'not to be worth' and 'not to care' to mean 'to be worth nothing', 'to care not at all' or 'not the least bit'. The most common are **straw, pin, fig, rap, hang, damn.** There are also some phrases, e.g. **two hoots, a tinker's cuss.** These words and phrases were chosen as typical of what was quite or almost worthless. (This would not apply today to **figs.**) **hang** and **damn** are formations connected with expletive verbs.

A *rap* was a counterfeit coin, worth about half a farthing, which passed current for a halfpenny in Ireland in the eighteenth century on account of the scarcity of genuine currency.

1010

not worth his salt. *not worth the salary he is paid;* or, loosely, *not competent, not efficient.* The earliest record of the expression given by the *Oxford Book of English Proverbs* is its use in 1830 in Captain Marryat's *The King's Own.* (OO)

1011

wring one's withers. *cause one concern or distress.* The 'withers' are the ridge between a horse's shoulder-blades, which can be made painful—'wrung'—by e.g. an ill-fitting saddle or collar. The common collocation of the verb 'wrung' with 'withers' in this phrase is due to a passage in *Hamlet*, III, ii, 255:

Let the galled jade wince, our withers are unwrung.

1012

the writing on the wall. *an event that shows impending misfortune or disaster.* The allusion is to Belshazzar's feast in Babylon (*Daniel*, 5). 'In that night', says the Bible story, 'was Belshazzar, King of the Chaldeans, slain.'

1013

the wrong end of the stick: see 289.

1014

to be on the wrong tack. *in an approach to, explanation of, interpretation of, a matter, to take a line that does not lead in the right direction, and will therefore not reach a sound conclusion.* The metaphor is based on a nautical use of the word 'tack' in sailing. It can be, but is rarely, used with reference to being 'on the right tack'. In a sailing race there may be a right or a wrong tack (direction) for a boat to take that affects its progress towards the point for which it is making, caused by currents or by different directions and strength of winds due to the configuration of the land.

1015

You can whistle for (it or that). *There is not the slightest chance of getting* (*it* or *that*). Brewer mentions an old superstition that when a ship was becalmed a wind might be raised by whistling.

1016

apostrophe 's'. The usage, a rather ungrammatical misusage, here is of only a second of two possessive words of a compound noun e.g. **Bryant and May's** instead of **Bryant's and May's.**

1017

billet. noun. (1) assignation of soldier to board and lodging. (2) wood cut to length for fuel.

1018

Every bullet has its billet. Every missile of this sort has its destination for those whose death has been assigned by Providence.

1019

to die in the last ditch. resist to the last extreme.

INDEX

The references are to the numbers of the articles (not to pages).

In the body of the book the idioms, either within the general arrangement, or at three points where a section of them is classified under special headings, appear in alphabetical order according to the first significant word in each. Consequently they there themselves automatically supply one index based on that principle. The list of words that now follows is supplementary. In this to have given the first significant word in each idiom would have been repetitive. Instead, there is given another, and sometimes more than one other, significant word, to provide an alternative means to that in the List of Idioms of finding the number of the article wherein a required idiom is treated of which the first significant word is not remembered.

above, 388
account, 864, 865
ace, 387
Adam, 541
all, 5–19, 542
alone, 555
amok (amuck), 747
anchor, 793
another, 798, 810
answer, 542
anything, 576
apostrophe 's', 1016
apple, 21–3
applecart, 977
arm, 566
as, 25, 177
ascendant, 874
ashes, 754
Atkins, 955
Augean, 139

baby, 519
back, 94, 246, 341, 440
bad, 29, 78, 458
bag, 32, 247
baggage, 32
baked, 594
balance, 481
ball, 33, 414, 415
balmy, 590
barmy, 590
barrel, 564
basket, 18
bats, 591
be, 684
bed, 47, 428
bedrock, 422
beer, 50, 822
bell, 733, 835
below, 409
belt, 409
berth, 436
better, 212, 443
big, 55, 677
bill, 372
billet, 1017

bird, 56, 538, 563
biscuit, 908
bit, 57, 904
bite, 58, 59, 489, 973
black, 61, 78, 681
blanket, 85, 985
bless, 935
Blimp, 152
block, 137
blot, 65, 66
blow, 68, 778
blue, 69–74
bluff, 389
blush, 346
Bo, 766
board, 388, 401, 441
boat, 108, 757
boiling, 533
bold, 310
bolt, 74, 800
bone, 75, 76, 338, 584
bonnet, 48, 942
book, 77–82
boot, 84, 507
bow, 260, 261, 974
box, 758
brain, 179
brand (bran), 89
brass, 166, 836
bread, 90, 126, 543
breadth, 465
break, 91–7, 103, 571
brick, 164, 265, 577
bright, 159
bring, 77, 99–101, 410
brown, 105
brush, 760, 959
buck, 396
bucket, 225
bug, 55
bull, 144, 725, 905
bullet, 1018
bury, 112, 113, 490
bus, 607
bush, 44
bushel, 512
butter, 90, 543
butterfly, 91
bygones, 115
cackle, 196
Cain, 720
cake, 272, 908
call, 389, 681, 860
can, 907
candle, 109, 385, 631
candlestick, 204
canoe, 643
cap, 116–19
card, 392–4, 398, 399, 405, 841
care, 1009
carry, 121–3, 907
cart, 124, 709
cast, 125–7, 293, 384
cat, 244–5, 247–9, 251, 252
catch, 130, 850
Cerberus, 834
chalk, 133–5
change, 424
chapter, 437
Charles, 539
Charybdis, 774
chase, 989
cheek, 842
cheese, 133
cherry, 973
chestnut, 694
chew, 59
chicken, 172
China, 136
choice, 516
circle, 866
circuit, 801
clock, 637
close, 140, 141, 755
cloth, 193
clutch, 131
coal, 121, 487, 494
coat, 193, 962

cock, 144–49
cocked, 540
cockle, 510
coin, 656
coincidence, 566
cold, 67, 150, 151, 435
colour, 153–62
come, 8, 100, 153, 163–70, 410
comfort, 150
comforter, 526
compliment, 554
conscience, 13
contention, 75
copy-book, 66
corn, 963
corner, 521
counter, 611
country, 558
courage, 268
court, 376
Coventry, 782
cow, 170
cracking, 421
crew, 380
cricket, 383
crocodile, 173
crook, 522
crop, 618
cropper, 163
cross, 174, 175, 256
crust, 920, 978
cry, 178, 327, 1001
cupboard, 181, 817
Damocles, 897
dash, 185
day, 205–13
dead, 42, 214–18
deaf, 966
deal, 722, 855
death, 223, 224, 228
deep, 230, 232, 282
description, 52
deuce, 233
devil, 232–5, 661
diamond, 738
Dick, 954
die, 1019
difference, 846
different, 133, 810
dirty, 981
discord, 22
ditch, 1019
do, 237
dog, 238–44, 249, 252, 270
Domini, 20
done, 19
door, 549, 565, 808, 1002
door-nail, 214
dot, 256, 809
dovecotes, 359
down, 164–7, 257–9, 572
dozen, 814, 915
drake, 670
draw, 309
drawer, 957
dried, 187
drive, 100
duck, 670
due, 235, 438
dust, 297, 369
dusty, 267
ear, 356, 492, 636, 687, 785, 966, 1003
earth, 167, 269, 751
eat, 240, 271–5
edge, 787
egg, 18, 29, 537, 621
Egyptians, 847
elbow(s), 276, 277, 609
elephant, 987
end, 39, 60, 109, 279–90, 321
enter, 524
errand, 361
escutcheon, 65
even, 964
eye, 6, 9, 23, 292–300, 463
eyelashes, eyelids, 480
face, 191, 303–20

fair, 213, 381, 855
fairy, 322
fall, 296, 323–6, 730
false, 154, 160, 382
Fanny, 686
fast, 397
favour, 183
feather, 116, 329–36
fence, 165, 813
fiddle, 671
fight, 149, 340, 341
figure, 186
fine, 190, 332, 333, 685
finger, 107, 343–5
fire, 328, 447, 479, 494, 525, 527, 694, 788, 825
fish, 178, 264, 347–53
fit, 18
flat, 355, 552, 928
flesh, 349, 358, 682, 937
floor, 1000
fly, 153, 177, 360
follow, 391
fool, 361
foot, 33, 151, 325, 365–72
forelock, 910
foul, 324
four, 17, 857
fowl, 349
free, 375
French, 900
fruit, 218
fry, 350, 527, 823
full, 333
funeral, 377
funk, 69

gaff, 68
gaga, 593
gain, 570
gallery, 673
GAMES, 219, 380–418
garden, 550
gauntlet, 750, 939
general, 132
get, 166, 246, 420–30, 477, 617, 858, 921
ghost, 221
gift-horse, 568
gilt, 906
gingerbread, 906
give, 155, 221, 235, 893
glove, 472
gnat, 887
go, 34, 100, 222, 242, 282, 439–455, 768
goat, 425, 783
good, 79, 311, 333, 349, 458, 941
goose, 7, 537, 766, 989
Gordian, 197
gorge, 585
grain, 459, 913
grapes, 838
grass, 365, 461, 826
grease, 276
grief, 168
grim, 223
grind, 28
grindstone, 532
grist, 8, 101
ground, 93, 445
grow, 365
Grundy, 610
gun, 844, 881

had, 485
hair, 284, 465–9
half, 814
half-baked, 594
hammer, 439
hand, 117, 400, 402, 471–6, 476, 554, 990
handle, 433
hang, 223, 427, 477–83
ha'porth, 848
hare, 574
Harry, 954

hat, 30, 486, 540, 902, 917
hatch, 172
hatchet, 112
hatter, 573
have, 151, 272, 303, 343, 392, 429, 473, 507–9, 595, 596, 604, 669, 842
hay, 579, 580
head, 58, 111, 449, 492–505, 539
heart, 273, 507–11
heel, 2, 258, 492, 535
heir, 358
hell, 731
Herod, 642
herring, 349, 724
high, 333, 729
hit, 495, 514, 515, 861
hog, 446
hold, 519, 520, 631
hole, 521, 854
hollow, 45
home, 100, 170
hoof, 807
hope, 373
horns, 905
horse, 42, 196, 203, 565, 568, 709, 729, 884
hot, 67, 892
hour, 278, 824
house, 99, 393
humble, 271

i's, 256
ice, 95, 816
iron, 524, 525, 892
it, 582

Joan, 202
joint, 627
juice, 880
jump, 251, 527

Kalends, 462
keep, 305, 415, 497, 498, 529, 532, 533, 1002
kettle, 348, 681
kick, 225, 535, 536
knot, 197
lamb, 933
lance, 92, 375
large, 114
last, 1019
laurel, 728
lay, 549, 707
lead, 550, 625, 896
leaf, 82, 83
leather, 731
leave, 900
lecture, 184
left-handed, 554
leg, 84, 370, 379, 434, 545, 629, 691
lend, 155
let, 243, 247, 365, 555
letter, 90, 216
lid, 710
lie, 243, 549, 777
life, 239, 244
light, 512, 871
like, 149, 156, 164, 223, 264, 322, 557, 725, 819, 852
lily, 648
line, 49, 418, 558, 723, 809
linen, 981
lion, 41, 502, 559–62
lip, 529
little, 563
loaf, 978
loin, 432
long, 102, 134, 261, 309, 566, 567, 828
loose, 279, 595, 596, 604
lose, 307, 493, 499, 570, 571
loss, 194
lot, 31
Lothario, 419
love, 181

luck, 572, 680
lucky, 935
lump, 557
lurch, 395

mackerel, 850
madness, 598
make, 283, 284, 500, 575–87, 636
manger, 238
march, 876
March, 574
mare, 792
marines, 931
mark, 418, 763
market, 266
mast, 157
matter, 605, 820, 858
meal, 856
measure, 175
meet, 283
men, 217
mended, 552
midnight, 110
midsummer, 598
mild, 262
mill, 8, 101
mincemeat, 583
mind, 606, 950
miss, 596, 604, 607, 613
moment, 690
money, 156, 458, 744
monkey, 426
monster, 463
monument, 654
moon, 72
mouth, 86, 259, 306, 471, 502, 508, 568, 589, 884
much, 669
music, 318
mutton, 215

nail, 157, 495, 611, 657, 926
necessity, 575
neck, 88, 96, 423, 616–20
nest, 331, 621
nettle, 460
new, 83, 93, 843
Newcastle, 121
nice, 685
nines, 263
nineteen, 915
no, 424, 825
nose, 191, 532, 625–8
nostril, 98
not, 248, 267, 365, 467, 629–37, 1009, 1010
nothing, 620
number, 209, 951

oar, 728
oats, 839
off, 158, 504, 514, 515, 929, 948
oil, 110, 683, 891
ointment, 360
Oliver, 735
once, 72
one, 14, 443, 528, 538, 814
oneself, 53, 169
open, 300, 388
order, 21
'osses, 196
other, 84, 306, 350, 814
out, 257
out-Herod, 642
outs, 532
over, 10

P's, 606
pain, 644–7
pair, 798
pale, 649
palm, 40, 650
pamby, 612
pan, 354, 527
Parker, 628
pass, 176, 211, 226, 396
passage, 56

passing, 227
patch, 630
path, 550, 559, 688
Paul, 734
paw, 245
pay, 234, 626, 656–61, 734
peace, 666, 667
pearl, 127
peg, 854, 899
Peru, 136
penalties, 647
petard, 518
peter, 662
Peter, 734
pick, 76, 571, 663
pickle, 685
pie, 21, 271, 343
pig, 113
pikestaff, 668
pile, 622
pill, 431
pillar, 413
pinch, 664, 799
pipe, 666, 708
piper, 659
piping, 667
pitch, 714
place, 204, 509
plate, 669
play, 36, 233, 381–3, 397, 398, 406, 411, 670–4
plough, 474, 676
plumes, 87
pocus, 517
point, 123, 890
poke, 113
post, 413
pot, 450, 533, 677–81
potty, 600
pour, 683, 719
power, 609, 684
praise, 200
pretty, 685, 686
Pry, 655
public, 981
pudding, 275
pup, 831
purse, 636
put, 160, 246, 310, 311, 366, 367, 399, 474, 502, 627, 637, 695–712

Q's, 606
question, 51
quick, 198

rag, 725
raw, 722
read, 322, 723
reap, 840
rebuking, 762
record, 97
red, 349, 724–7
reed, 103
riband (ribbon), 71
right, 165, 495, 509
ring, 587, 733
riot, 749
rise, 585
roast, 743
robin, 739
rock, 422
roll, 415, 736, 784
Roman, 237
Rome, 237
rope, 291, 544, 737
rosa, 894
rose, 47
rot, 956
rough, 199, 738
roughshod, 732
round, 739, 740, 854
roundabout, 570
rub, 250, 412, 741
Rubicon, 176
ruin, 717
rumple, 336
run, 188, 503, 567, 744–52

safety, 411
sail, 755, 912
salt, 756, 913, 1010
same, 757–60
sanctity, 641
sand, 111, 676, 752
say, 454, 764–9,–789
scatty, 601
school, 930
scratch, 380, 410
screw, 595, 702
screwy, 602
'scutcheon, 65
sea, 5, 218
second, 671, 974
see 156, 212, 251, 294, 635, 727, 775–80
sepulchre, 988
set, 119, 313, 368, 707, 784–88
seven, 815
shaft, 652
shake, 369, 791
shape, 556
share, 562
shave, 614
sheep, 61, 293, 783, 1005
sheet, 793, 873
shilling, 192
shine, 580, 909
ship, 848
shoe, 217, 796–9
shop, 916
shorn, 933
shot, 652
shoulder, 435, 707, 885
shrift, 802
shy, 340
side, 62, 165, 428, 543, 701
silk, 636
silver, 86
sin, 762
skin, 919
skittles, 50
slam, 808
slate, 596, 700
sleep, 243, 819, 820
sleeve, 392, 511, 547
smoke, 281, 708, 825
snake, 773, 826
sneeze, 634
snuff, 829
soap, 830
soft, 603, 830
song, 833, 895
soonest, 551
soul, 524
sound, 322, 835, 836
sow, 636, 639, 840
Spain, 128
span, 843
spanner, 938
spite, 191
spoke, 698
sponge, 849, 945
spoon, 86
spur, 991
square, 15, 853–68
squarely, 861, 862
squib, 201
stable, 139, 565
stand, 284, 370, 629, 871, 873
star, 874, 935
stay, 712
steal, 565, 876, 877
step, 371, 878, 879
stick, 174, 289, 881
stiff, 529
stinking, 178
stock, 564
stone, 503, 538, 553, 736, 784
stool, 323
story, 144
straight, 305, 884–6
strain, 887, 890
straw, 131, 546, 577
street, 588, 715, 888, 889

stride, 901
strike, 100
string, 693, 797, 974
study, 104
suit, 81, 391
sun, 580
Sunday, 608
sure, 147
swan, 7, 895
sweep, 138, 401
swim, 811
swine, 127
swing, 248, 570, 896
sword, 175, 897

T, t, 256, 715
table, 399, 403, 740
tack, 166, 1014
tail, 493, 500
tale, 322, 930
tape, 726
tar, 760, 848, 959
Tartar, 130
task, 812, 911
tat, 953
tea, 180
teacup, 883
team, 380
tear, 173
tell, 563, 928–32
terms, 171
test, 3
tether, 286
Thames, 788
that, 27, 949, 975
there, 11, 12
thick, 57, 64, 448
thin, 288, 448, 816
thing, 528, 615
thread, 478, 571, 663
throat, 946
throw, 125, 297, 315, 402, 939, 942, 944, 945
thrust, 946
thumb, 742, 947, 972
thunder, 63, 877
tile, 604
time, 211, 653, 667, 910, 950, 951
tip, 886
tiptoe, 952
tit, 953
toe, 229, 417, 418
token, 759
Tommy, 955
ton, 164
tongs, 439
tongue, 842
too, 525, 669
tooth, 125, 787, 806, 904, 919–926
top, 819, 957
topsy-turvy, 958
traces, 536
tree, 38, 464, 635
trick, 486
troubled, 353, 683
true, 73, 162
trump, 404–8
tune, 810
turn, 83, 229, 403, 408, 467, 505, 964–71
turvy, 958
two, 174, 320, 323. 538, 711, 973, 974

unturned, 553
up, 16, 34, 298, 319, 386, 674
upper, 529, 977

venture, 260
verse, 437
victory, 713
virtue, 575

wagon, 35, 982
walk, 146
wall, 341, 452, 503, 1012

warm, 258, 510
water, 64, 126, 347, 353, 447, 498, 520, 683, 982
way, 189, 250, 444, 686
wear, 309, 511
wedge, 288
weight, 692
well, 398, 555
went, 34
were, 25
west, 222
wheel, 91, 698, 707, 986
whip, 473
whirlwind, 840
white, 335, 873, 987, 988
whole, 446
wide, 436
widow, 461
wig, 677
wild, 839, 989
wildfire, 853
win, 493, 990, 991
wind, 429, 430, 482, 721, 755, 778, 832, 840, 912, 933
windmill, 942
wink, 374
withers, 1011
wolf, 944, 1001–6
wood, 635
wood-pile, 622
word, 274
work, 938
world, 54
wormwood, 378
worse, 37
worth, 385, 1009, 1010
wrong, 38, 85, 250, 371, 428, 1014

years, 255